I0120740

John Ednie Brown

A Practical Treatise on Tree Culture in South Australia

John Ednie Brown

A Practical Treatise on Tree Culture in South Australia

ISBN/EAN: 9783337314989

Printed in Europe, USA, Canada, Australia, Japan

Cover: Foto ©Lupo / pixelio.de

More available books at **www.hansebooks.com**

A PRACTICAL TREATISE

ON

TREE CULTURE

IN

SOUTH AUSTRALIA.

By J. E. BROWN, F.L.S.,

Conservator of Forests for the Government of South Australia.

WITH NUMEROUS ILLUSTRATIONS BY J. W. LOVE.

ADELAIDE :
PRINTED AND LITHOGRAPHED BY E. SPILLER, GOVERNMENT PRINTER, NORTH-TERRACE.

1881.

C.T

Published under the authority of the Forest Board
of South Australia.

H. D. MELVILLE, Secretary.

Adelaide, April 4th, 1881.

Forest Board Office, Adelaide, South Australia,

April 4th, 1881.

The Board has much pleasure in assisting the Conservator in giving this little work to the public. Its preparation evidences ability and zeal; its compilation has not been allowed to interfere with the Conservator's important and widely-spread duties; and its production may be accepted as an indication of Mr. Brown's genuine interest in Arboriculture, which should be eminently satisfactory to the public and to the Government, whose officer he is.

G.. W. GOYDER, *Chairman,*

B. T. FINNISS, J.P.,

WILLIAM BARBER, Col., J.P.,

RICHARD SCHOMBURGK Dr. Ph.

GEORGE McEWIN, J.P.,

Members of the Board

Contents.

—>⊂≎>✕⚡✦⊂≎<—

INTRODUCTION.

ARBORICULTURE, according to the common acceptation of the word, is the art of planting and rearing trees and shrubs; but in the opinion of the most learned *savans* of the age it is now also looked upon as one of the most important of the many *sciences* which regulate the economic and hygienic affairs of nations.

It is now generally admitted by all enlightened people that trees play a very important part in the general prosperity of any country, and that, by the amount of attention paid by its inhabitants to their cultivation, so may the physical and intellectual standard of the people be estimated. As our surroundings become physically more perfect, so in the same ratio do we become morally better. As one proof of this we have only to refer to the case of some of the ancient nations in Asia, such as Persia, Palestine, and Syria. In the early and most prosperous days of these countries, the inhabitants paid very great attention to the rearing of both fruit and timber trees, and, in consequence, their agriculture was highly productive, and all classes were prosperous. What is now the condition of these once fertile regions? It is this: their forests have been long ago destroyed; their fields are now, comparatively speaking, parched and unremunerative to the cultivators, and therefore agriculture is neglected, and their people have sunk into poverty and wretchedness; while the civilisation which once regulated their affairs has fallen with them, and left them in the condition of semi-barbarism in which they now are found.

It is evident from the records which we now possess that the planting of trees was understood and practised in the early days of the world's history, though of course on a more primitive and less methodical plan than is now done in these modern and more enlightened days. Not to speak of what must have been done in tree planting in the early days to which Holy Writ has reference, but of which no positive proof has been handed down to us, we find from the earliest historians that the Greeks and Romans were great arboriculturists, and made wonderful steps in their time in the rearing of trees, both for ornamental and economic purposes.

It is supposed that the propagation of trees and the introduction of new species into Europe began about the fifteenth century, from which time until the present day various works on arboriculture have been published. At first these were necessarily of the most primitive character, both in style, substance, and knowledge; now they are of the most scientific and reliable kind. At the present day we find that tree planting in Britain, Germany, France, and other divisions of the Continent of Europe, has become a very important industry; and that, viewed in the light of a commercial transaction alone, it ranks amongst the foremost of the rural industries of the political economy of these countries. Perhaps within the last eighty or one hundred years more has been done towards planting by landed proprietors in the old world than in any former period of its history. This has arisen from many causes, the chief of these being a better knowledge of the art in all its detail management, resulting in a surer and more paying return; the introduction from various parts of the world of quick-growing and valuable species of trees; the general recognition of the now well-established fact that trees exercise a very marked and valuable influence on the climatic and hygienic conditions of a country; and that so many establishments have been started for the sale of forest trees, thereby causing keen competition, and consequently reasonable prices for plants.

Of late years, from various causes incidental to the rise and prosperity of the country, the colonies of Australasia have awakened to the necessity for a proper conservation of their forests, and planting of woodlands on the otherwise unwooded portions of the respective provinces, in order to the permanent good and well-being of the country. Victoria and New Zealand have each given birth to Acts of Parliament on the subject, but these have not been properly carried out. Queensland and New South Wales are now agitating the matter; but it remained for South Australia to have the honor of being the first Australian colony to establish a system of forestry in her midst.

The originator of the scheme was Mr. Krichauff, M.P., who, in the session of 1871, called for a return eliciting information from persons resident in the different districts of the colony, in regard to the supply, preservation, and culture of forests. The answers were summarised and prepared by Dr. Schomburgk, the Director of the Botanic Gardens.

Subsequent to this return, Mr. Krichauff introduced, and successfully passed, in the House of Assembly, in 1873, "An Act to encourage the planting of Forest Trees," which provided for the payment by Government of two pounds per acre for every acre planted by a landowner in certain districts of the colony, according to certain defined conditions.

During the same session, a "Report on Forest Reserves" was laid on the table of the House, which had been prepared for the Honorable the Commissioner of Crown Lands by G. W. Goyder, Esq., the Surveyor-General. This report made suggestions for the proclamation of certain portions of the country as forest reserves, and dealt exhaustively with recommendations regarding the formation of a Department of Forests.

In 1875 a Bill was brought in by Mr. Krichauff, and passed, intituled "An Act to make provision for the appointment of a Forest Board, and for other purposes." In this Act certain districts pointed out by Mr. Goyder were defined as forest reserves.

During the session of 1876 a short Act was passed to amend certain portions of the Forest Board Act; and "The Forest Trees Act," under which the present operations of the Forest Board are being carried out, was passed in 1878. The latter Act consolidates and amends all the laws in the colony relating to forest trees, and embraces the different matters provided for in all the three Acts previously quoted.

Forestry is a branch of rural economy not so easily defined in all its parts as farming is, and this chiefly from its crops requiring a considerable number of years to test the results of any experiments that may be made in it. The subject of forest management is a long and broad one, requiring an age of observation and experience in anyone to understand the effects of certain modes of operations. In old and long-established countries, such as those of Europe, where the original forests have for the greater part disappeared many generations ago, and new ones been planted, forestry is taught both theoretically and practically, and is, generally speaking, well understood by all classes concerned in the rural economy of the respective countries. On the other hand, in these colonies the inhabitants hitherto have been principally engaged in the destruction of their trees in order to make way for the tilling of the land they occupy, and are, as a rule, unacquainted with even the rudiments of forestry, and are quite at a loss how to proceed should they wish to plant a few trees on their holdings. Now that the thinking and prudent portion of the landowners of the country are alive to the important functions which trees play in our midst, and are already showing a strong disposition to form plantations on their estates, but are often deterred from doing so from want of knowledge of the subject, I have thought it incumbent upon myself to come forward with this concise and practical work on forest management generally, with the view of supplying what I feel is a much-felt want in the colony, and thereby enabling the landowners of our community with its use to improve their properties by planting trees on them, both for ornament and use, and to become their own foresters with every reasonable chance of success.

At first it was the author's intention to issue this work in the usual way through a publisher, but seeing difficulties in the way of its general distribution, the matter was laid before the Forest Board, offering the MS. on the condition that it be printed at the expense of the Government and issued gratuitously. This suggestion the members of the Forest Board at once adopted.

With these few introductory remarks the author commits his small work to the public, and trusts that many will find useful hints in its pages; and if only a few will be induced thereby to plant trees on their land, he will feel more than repaid for the labor expended upon it.

Forest Board Office, Adelaide,
      March, 1881.

TREE CULTURE IN SOUTH AUSTRALIA.

TREE CULTURE IN SOUTH AUSTRALIA.

CHAPTER I.

Importance of Conserving Forests and Forming Plantations in South Australia.

IN nearly all the countries of Europe and in India, forest management is now generally well understood, each having a systematic forest economy of its own, modified to suit the existing peculiarities of the region it occupies, and each carrying out with rigor the arrangements laid down for the development of this branch of its natural resources, all keeping in view to carefully preserve the older portions of their forest crops, and to plant and rear young ones to come in for use as their supplies of the old crops become exhausted.

In South Australia we have a large and valuable agricultural country, but with the undoubted drawback of having only a limited *ligneous* flora. Our forests occupy but a very small percentage of our area, and even much of what is termed " timbered country" is under trees of an inferior class. While, however, our country does not compare with many other portions of the globe in the possession of valuable forest products, it is more than satisfactory to note that it is vastly superior to many others as a field for the development of systematic forestry— whether as to soil, climate, or extent of field to operate on.

As in all newly-settled countries, so it has been here, and is yet to some extent in places, the natural forests have been wantonly destroyed. Happily, however, for the future prosperity of the colony, a wise Government has taken steps, by the proclamation of certain districts as forest reserves, and by the establishment of a Forest Board, whereby a thorough system of conserving and planting is being undertaken upon them, to prevent the complete demolition of the natural forests, and at the same time introduce other species of trees which will produce valuable timber to future generations.

While, however, the Government is doing all it possibly can in the matter, this is not sufficient for the ultimate good and prosperity of the colony as a whole. Conserving and planting trees will and *must* become a universal industry in this country at no great distant day. To the landowners we must look for that general system of planting which will ultimately ameliorate the hot winds of our summers, increase and equalise our rainfall, and conduce to the increased products of our soil.

Why should a country such as this is, with its rich soil and general natural advantages, have to depend, as it now does, on foreign importations for a supply of even the commonest class of timber? There is no reason why it should be so, and yet it is humiliating to confess that at the present time but a very small proportion of the timber used in permanent works in the colony is from trees grown in the country.

If we have to rely upon foreign supplies for our timber now, what shall we do fifteen or twenty years hence, when our population shall have increased tenfold? At that time the demand for timber will be increased to an extent which we can have no idea of at the present time. Will the supply then be had from other countries? No. It is not in the common nature of things that this could be so, seeing that every civilised country is beginning to feel that it must increase its available supply of timber to meet the demands of its own growing requirements. Where, for instance, are the fine forests of Huon pine and Sydney cedar which produced such an unlimited supply of timber only a few years ago? These are getting pretty well swept away by the indiscriminate slaughter which has marked the mismanagement of these fine and valuable forest lands.

Then, from these facts it is evident that the only alternative is, South Australia must of necessity, like other countries, attend to conserve her existing supply of timber, and to plant extensively, in order to secure artificial crops to take the place of the old and matured ones as these become exhausted.

Apart altogether from the quantity of timber that is to provide for the domestic wants of the people, the important and increasing mining operations, which are here as yet but coming into existence, demand an extension of woodlands in order to support them in proper working condition as they gradually develop. I think it is safe to assert that ere many years pass the mining industry of South Australia will absorb vast quantities of timber, as it has already done when the copper mines were in full working order. It is, therefore, incumbent upon us to prepare for this, and to devise such measures as will secure a continuance of the supply of the timber required to carry on and develop a branch of industry which has already conduced so materially to our welfare as a colony.

Look, next in order, to the vast system of railways which is gradually being opened up in our midst. These will require a vast quantity of timber annually for their proper maintenance. At present much of the timber used in our railways is imported from the other colonies, but as these supplies are being gradually exhausted, we must soon look within ourselves to keep good the supply.

Then look at the very large amount of fencing which is done in this country. At present this more than consumes all the available timber growing in the colony; indeed, in some districts the farmers cannot even get enough wood for this one purpose within easy distance of their holdings, and have to be content with very unsatisfactory fences made of scrub timber and brushwood. Here, then, we have another very important incentive to planting, and as, in the ordinary course of affairs, the demand for fencing materials will increase as the resources of the colony become developed and the population increases, it becomes more than ever necessary that the woodlands of the country be increased to such an extent as will ensure a sufficiency of fencing materials for all time to come.

I am, moreover, of opinion that it is the duty of every landowner here to grow trees himself in such quantity as will supply him with all the timber he may require for fencing and domestic purposes.

These statements are enough to satisfy any thinking person as to the great importance of conserving the existing forests, and planting with young trees the waste and other lands of this fine country, so that the supply of timber may be secured under all circumstances.

But it is not only the supplying of the various industries of the country with necessary timber that is to be had in view in the preservation of our old forests and planting young plantations, but the present cry for an advanced state of agriculture here demands that a skilful and well-defined system of forest operations be conducted over all for its special benefit.

It is well known to all who have given their attention to the improvement of lands in any country that the formation of plantations is one of the chief means to this end, and that without a due proportion of these no permanent improvement in this way can ever be attained. Trees are the grand regulators of climate and improvers of the soil, under all circumstances and conditions.

There is no doubt but that the cause of so much waste land, so to speak, being found in the central parts of this continent, is attributable to the want of trees to give it shelter. Will anyone say that the great dry wastes at present existing in this country cannot be improved in climate and in soil by a judicious planting of proper sorts of trees on them? I believe that no one acquainted with the general laws of nature affecting such subjects will deny that these wastes may be made fertile, agriculturally, and made the field for the happy homes of thousands of settlers, by a judicious system of planting, so as to protect them from the local causes which render them at present unfit for habitation and settlement.

Besides, has not the neglect of judicious planting of trees been conducive to the present unprofitable state of many of the farms in the older-settled parts of the colony—farms which have no doubt been exhausted by excessive cropping, but which, had they been protected by the shade and shelter of skilfully-laid-out plantations, would have been vastly more remunerative, even with the defective system of farming under which they have been placed, than they are now? Hence the necessity there is for every landed proprietor in this colony to plant a certain extent of his subject with trees.

CHAPTER II.

The Benefits which would accrue to the Soil and Climate of the Colony from a General System of Tree Planting.

THAT large bodies of trees have a direct influence on the atmospheric changes of a district or country is, I think, in these days of so much statistical and other reliable information, now a recognised fact. If we look back and examine ancient, mediæval, and modern history, we there find many very noted examples of decrease of rains, dried up rivers, extended deserts, and depleted populations, simply from the clearing of extensive forests; while again, on the other hand, it has been observed that where large tracts of country have been laid under a crop of trees, and which, previous to this having been done, were designated dry and comparatively unproductive parts, small streams of water have been found where none formerly existed, and the general nature of the districts has been improved to such an extent that they have become highly favorable for agricultural purposes, and hence more able to sustain an increased population. I now note a few of the influences which would flow to this country by extensive planting on its surface.

Trees would give Shelter.—In the agricultural parts of this colony, especially in the Northern Areas, where extensive tracts of most excellent country are open to every blast of wind which blows, it is self-evident that the planting of belts of trees in different directions through them would have a most beneficial influence on the crops which are produced upon the ground. The direct result of such belts would be that the hot winds, which at present are the scourge of the country so far as their effects upon vegetation are concerned, would, if they were not in time subdued altogether, be at all events considerably softened by coming in contact with the cooler atmosphere arising from the damper surface of the ground shaded by the trees, and therefore pass harmlessly over the country; and thus the crops would not only be more certain, but would grow more luxuriantly, and consequently the yield would be proportionately larger. Again, another important result which would arise to the agricultural community from the planting of trees on the plains would be, that shelter would be given to stock both from the hot winds of summer and the storms and cold blasts of winter.

Our Soil would be Improved.—To have good agricultural soil, we must have a large proportion of vegetable matter in it. With this fact before us, it is at once apparent that the annual deposit of the leaves and bark of trees on the ground which they occupy, must enrich it to a very considerable extent. This vegetable matter becomes decomposed and amalgamated with the soil, and thus the surface soil becoming of a porous and absorbent nature, the rain is retained and stored up for the use in dry weather of the plants growing upon it. Moreover, on soils of a stiff and clayey character, the roots of trees planted upon them would penetrate and ramify in all directions through them, and thus not only act as a subsoiler in breaking up the hard pan below for the easier entrance of the small fibrous roots of cereals and other agricultural crops, but at the same time would open up a way for the percolation and retention of the water which would otherwise flow along the surface and find its level elsewhere, without being retained for the after and gradual use of the plants growing upon them.

Less Evaporation would take place.—It is, perhaps, almost superfluous to remark, that very great evaporation takes place all over the colony at all seasons of the year, from the thoroughly exposed character of the country generally to the full power of the sun's rays. In consequence of this, what rain falls upon the ground is, almost as soon as it reaches the ground, again taken up into the air by evaporation, without being retained in the soil for the use of the crops growing upon it. Even on those parts of the country which are under indigenous forests, from the scattered and generally sparse crop of trees constituting these, together with the peculiarly characteristic feature of the Australian trees, affording but little shade to the ground—owing to upright habit of the foliage—evaporation goes on in a very rapid manner. It is chiefly to these causes alone that I attribute the fact of there being so few never-failing creeks and rivers in this colony. Now, were there judiciously laid-out plantations all over the country, and the trees constituting them being at such distances apart and of such kinds as would effectually shade the ground from the sun, and prevent evaporation to a large extent from these parts—or at least in a much slower manner than is done at present—the rain would have time and opportunity to be absorbed into the ground, and by percolating to considerable depths, come out again at a lower level, and thus cause streams of water where none exist at present, and so on from place to place, keeping up a general degree of humidity to refresh and encourage the growth of vegetation.

On the other hand where forests have been felled, and the surface left exposed, great evaporation takes place; and the rainfall which formerly went to feed streams has been carried away, and these have in consequence dried up.

Destructive Floods would be avoided.—Sudden, and therefore damaging, floods, are characteristic features of the climate of this colony. This is to be expected, and can be easily accounted for. The surface of the country being very much exposed to the sun's rays, becomes baked and parched: and, in consequence, when heavy rains come on, the soil not being open and porous, these flow along the surface of the ground and accumulating in the hollows, rush downwards, causing inundation and ruin in their course.

B

To mitigate these floods very considerably there are two courses open to us, viz. :—1st, by an extended system of arable farming ; and 2nd, by planting large masses of trees.

First then, as to the benefits to be derived from more extensive tillage operations. It has been remarked to me that, of late years, not only has the rainfall in the colony been as much as it used to be when larger forests existed in the country than there are in it at the present time, but that even the floods are not now so extensive as they were. These facts are accounted for thus :—Now that considerable portions of the country have been put under the plough, and the soil become broken up and rendered more porous by cultivation, the results are :—(1.) The rains are absorbed by the loose soil as they fall, and, being percolated gradually through it to considerable depths, are retained and diffused over the country in small streams. (2.) The water being absorbed by the soil, more vapour is generated in the surrounding neighborhood, and consequently the air becomes more moist, and forms an attraction for rain clouds ; thus more rain falls upon the ground than formerly ; and (3), the rain being taken into the soil and given out gradually as explained above, the accumulation of large bodies of water by it when heavy showers take place is reduced to a minimum. Therefore, it will be found that as the country becomes more settled, and a greater extent of its surface is broken up, so in proportion will the chances of sudden floods be reduced.

Secondly, as to the effects which large masses of trees have in the mitigation of floods. These are (1) by the shelter and annual deposit of vegetable matter to the soil, this is rendered looser on the surface, and of a more absorbent nature, and thus when rains come the water is quickly taken into the ground, and is given off gradually in the form of a watery vapour, exhaled from the leaves of the trees, and by the means of small streams. In this way, in the immediate neighborhood of extensive tracts of forest country, the danger of sudden floods is very much diminished. As an illustration of the very absorbent nature of the soil which is shaded by trees, I would instance the extensive forests of Canada as a case in point, where I have seen it rain heavily for ten hours at a time, and still there would not be any appreciative rise in the rivers.' Here, then, we see that instead of a destructive flood arising, the rain was stored up in the earth for supply during dry weather. In the early days of American settlement, when the country was densely covered with forests, such a thing as a flood was but little known. Now, however, in those parts of the country where extensive clearances have taken place within the last century, floods of fearful magnitude occur, which are the means annually of sweeping off hundreds of lives and thousands of pounds' worth of property.

I cannot but quote here from an excellent essay written by an American lately on this subject.—" Now, a body of timber is especially adapted for the retention of the rainfall. Suppose twelve inches of water falls in an open country, and the same amount in a forest in twenty-four hours. In the former instance, though the ground may be dry, it is impossible for it to take in this amount—probably not more than four or six inches. Now multiply the area of the watered region by six inches, and you have a flood of fearful magnitude—especially if the country is rolling.

"Let the same amount fall in a forest. You watch it as it falls. Ten thousand leaves on every tree catch and hold the drops, and when they strike the ground there are six inches of leaf-mould, and the ground itself for a foot in depth is very porous, the leaves hold it till the ground drinks it in; the old rotten logs are all like sponges, and if the ground mulch cannot retain it, all the roots seem to build dams to obstruct it, and though so much rain has fallen the streams are hardly swollen. And now we see the design of this surface cistern. The water begins to ooze out by slow degrees, and when the streams of the open country have run themselves dry, and the ground is baked for the want of more rain, the wood-fed streams are in their full flow. The navigation of our finest rivers is already affected by thoughtless destruction of the forests. When will man learn that God made trees for more purposes than the lumber in them."

Our Rainfall would be Equalised.—In this colony, the climate of which is considered very dry, nearly as much rain falls within the twelve months as there falls within a same period in some countries which are really humid ones. In moist climates we find that on nearly three-fourths of the days of the year rain falls more or less. In this country, again, there are at least three-fourths of the twelve months which are entirely cloudless. And still the rainfall in both instances is not in like manner disproportionate so far as the total amounts for the year are concerned. These appear somewhat contradictory statements, but yet they are approximately correct for many cases which could be cited. The reason of the difference is not that the one country lies perhaps in the northern hemisphere and the other in the southern, or that the one may be 15 degrees nearer the equator than the other. No; the grand secret is that the country which has its rainfall spread over the whole year is thickly covered with trees, while in the case of our colony there is a very small proportion of its area occupied by forests. In two or three hours in this country as much rain will fall as would occupy two days steady drizzling in Great Britain.

More Rain would Fall.—That this would be the result of extensive planting in the colony there is no doubt. Reliable experiments and observations have shown clearly that this is invariably the case where large bodies of plantations are formed. To put the matter specifically we find (1) from the shade given by the trees the temperature of the earth is lowered; (2) the atmosphere hovering immediately above the trees is in consequence also lower than that in any part of the country adjoining which may be clear of vegetation; consequently it follows (3) that if hot winds blow over a plantation they will be cooled down and their moisture condensed upon coming in contact with the cool humid atmosphere hanging about the trees, and as their power of holding water in a condition of vapor is sensibly diminished in a certain ratio according to the fall of temperature, the result is a deposit on the ground of either rain, mist, or dew; and again (4) clouds containing vapour, which have

blown over dry ground heated by the sun, where the air is in consequence highly rarified and warmer than the clouds, these dissolve themselves and vanish; but should these clouds come in contact with the
cooler air above masses of trees they become overcharged with moisture,
and rain is the result.

Arid Tracts would be Improved.—We have seen that the planting of
large bodies of trees has the indirect influence of attracting rain-clouds
to the sites occupied by them, and that the atmosphere generally about
woodlands is in a continual state of moisture by transpiration from the
pores of the leaves, and by a certain amount of evaporation caused by
the heat of the sun. From this then, it will at once be seen, that by
planting arid tracts of land with properly proportioned belts of timber
here and there through them, the result is (1) lower temperature, (2)
arrest of hot winds, (3) shelter, (4) more frequent rains, and (5) a more
humid climate generally, thus making such tracts of country suitable for
agricultural purposes.

We would have a more Humid Climate.—A humid climate is a result and
component part of the whole system of the different influences of trees
upon climate which have already been explained. Water is sucked up
from the soil by the roots of the trees, and is exuded again in the form
of vapour from the stomachs on the back of the leaves; this rises into the
air and forms itself into clouds, and, if not deposited again on the ground
as rain by some counterbalancing atmospheric influence, is wafted
across the country, cooling the air and keeping up a supply of heavy
dews, which refresh and invigorate vegetable life. While again, the
humidity of the climate is maintained from the simple fact that the
green moist foliage of the trees constituting the forests has the well-
known tendency of preventing the increase of the sun's rays by radiation,
and thus reducing the chances of evaporation.

The Landscape would be Improved.—How different the contrast of
appearance between a country well stocked with trees and one bare of
these. The one looks clothed and picturesque, while the other has that
barren unproductive look which wearies the eye. Besides, in a commercial point of view alone, there exist strong arguments in favor of
trees. In the one case we have luxuriant crops, and fine arborous
retreats for stock, while in the other both stock and crops are subject to
all the changes of the weather, and look stunted and unhealthy.

Unhealthy Districts would be made Habitable.—Leaves of trees purify
the air by absolving the carbonic acid gas thrown into the air by the
breath of animals, and from the various forms of decomposition in nature.
They separate the carbon from the oxygen, retaining the first as food for
themselves and emitting the other for sustaining animal life.

In low-lying and swampy parts of a country, where rich organic mould
has been accumulating for thousands of years back, thereby promoting
a rank growth of aquatic vegetation, gases arise which have a very
deleterious effect upon animal life, and produce insidious and mortal
diseases. This is counteracted by the planting of certain kinds of trees;
notably that of the Tasmanian blue gum *(Eucalyptus globulus)*. There
is great room for the researches of science in this matter yet; but that

the effect is produced is a fact beyond dispute, and one which has of late years enabled certain districts in different parts of the world to be made habitable and productive.

From these statements, therefore, we see that a judicious distribution of plantations on an extensive scale would be the means of improving the climate of South Australia, of greatly increasing the quantity and quality of her agricultural products, and of promoting prosperity in every department of her industries. Will this not induce all who can do so to plant on their land? Let us be up and doing therefore. Every tree planted in a country such as this is like a nail in the construction of a house—one step further towards unity of parts and general strength in one grand whole.

CHAPTER III.

The Encouragement to Tree Culture in South Australia by Bonus from the Government.

In 1873, " An Act to Encourage the Planting of Trees " was passed by the South Australian Parliament. This Bill was introduced and successfully nursed by Mr. Krichauff, M.P., and was the first movement towards the formation of a department for the conservation and extension of forests in the colony, which followed shortly after. To Mr. Krichauff, therefore, the honor of this movement belongs.

Subsequently this Act was incorporated with the Forest Board Act of 1875, and now forms part of " The Forest Tree Act, No. 96 of 1878."

The clauses of this Act having special reference to the encouragement of tree planting are as follows :—

The Governor may from time to time, by Proclamation in the *Government Gazette*, declare any part of the province to be defined in such Proclamation to be a forest district, and fix a day to be named in such Proclamation on which this part of this Act shall come into operation in such district.

Until any such Proclamation as aforesaid, the provisions of this part of this Act shall apply only to the districts heretofore declared, and which are set forth in the schedule marked E.

Any person who shall, in accordance with any regulation in force under this Act, sow, plant, transplant, or cause to grow upon any land not less than five acres in extent and not being waste lands of the Crown, forest trees of the description mentioned in any such regulation, shall be entitled to receive an order in the form of schedule marked F, which order shall entitle such person to the amount of two pounds for every acre so planted, such amount to be credited to him on the purchase of any waste lands of the Crown in the province open for sale at auction or otherwise, or to be received in payment of the interest of the purchase-money if selected on credit or in payment of any rent due to the Government, but subject in every other respect to the laws and regulations for the time being in force regulating the sale and disposal of the waste lands of the Crown : Provided that the Commissioner of Crown Lands may refuse to grant any such order unless it shall be shown to his satisfaction that the land in respect of which such order is sought has been devoted to no other purpose, except for the purpose of protecting, planting, and gardening, as may be approved by the Commissioner, and except as provided in the 5th sub-paragraph of clause 3 of schedule II, than that of producing forest trees for at least two years, and that the trees on such land are in a vigorous and healthy condition, and that the land is securely fenced in against sheep and cattle.

Upon the certificate of any officer appointed under this part of this Act that the terms and conditions imposed by this Act have been complied with, the person to whom such certificate is given shall be entitled, on the production of such certificate to the Commissioner of Crown Lands, to receive an order for an amount to which such certificate shall prove him to be entitled.

Every such order shall be transferable, and shall be exercised within five years from the date hereof, and if not exercised within such period shall be absolutely null and void.

It shall be lawful for the holder of any order, if the sum of money named therein exceed fifty pounds, but not otherwise, to exercise such right wholly at one time, or from time to time (before the expiration of the period aforesaid), and to purchase, under such order, land in one parcel, or in more parcels than one; and whenever such order, whatever the amount thereof may be, shall be exercised by the purchase or selection of any such land as aforesaid, the holder of such order shall, at any time, when under the law in force regulating the sale of such lands he would be bound to pay any deposit, interest, rent, or purchase-money, if such purchase had been made under such law alone, and not under this Act, produce such order to the person to whom such deposit, interest, rent, or purchase-money may be payable; and such person shall thereupon note by endorsement on such order the sum of money which would be payable by such holder as such deposit, interest, rent, or purchase-money as aforesaid, and shall also give to the holder of the order a receipt or certificate in the like form and to the like effect as such holder would be entitled to receive if he had paid in cash the sum so endorsed; and such receipt or certificate shall have the same force and effect as if the holder of such certificate had paid such sum so endorsed as aforesaid : Provided, however, that when the order has been fully exercised it shall be given up to the Treasurer.

No land once planted shall entitle the owner to more than one order in respect of such land.

Any person holding a lease from the Crown for pastoral purposes may give written notice to the Commissioner of Crown Lands that he wishes to sow, plant, or transplant forest trees on any tract of land not being less than twenty acres, on the land held by him on lease, and in such notice shall define the number of trees on each acre, and the description of trees which he intends to sow, plant, or transplant, and state the amount of compensation which he expects in case of resumption; and if no objection is raised by the Commissioner within six months after the giving of such notice, all trees sown, planted, or transplanted in pursuance of any such notice which shall at the time of resumption be in a vigorous and healthy state, at least ten feet high, and securely fenced against sheep and cattle, shall be an improvement for which compensation shall be given if such land is resumed : Provided that in no case more than two pounds shall be paid for every acre sown, planted, transplanted, and resumed.

The following regulations relating to the planting and preservation of forest trees were, in accordance with clause 29 of " The Forest Trees Act," made and issued by the Forest Board on the 16th October, 1876 :—

Persons planting trees and wishing to avail themselves of the provisions of clause 22 of this Act, may claim the orders referred to in such clause, not earlier than two years nor later than five years after the date of planting, such claim to be made in writing and addressed to the Secretary of the Forest Board.

Persons planting trees as above and maintaining them in good order, will be entitled to the orders specified in the Act at the end of five years from the date of such planting, on the certificate of the Conservator of Forests, or other officer appointed by the Governor to report on such planting, that all the conditions of the Act and of these regulations, have been complied with.

Conditions to be complied with by persons claiming orders :—

Distances at which Trees to be planted.—Trees must be planted not more than sixteen (16) feet apart.

Size of Blocks.—Blocks planted to be not less than five acres in area, and if strips of land are planted in form of shrubbery they must be not less than 100ft. wide.

Description of Trees.—Trees to be planted must consist of the following :—

Eucalypti, except dwarf varieties	Chestnut	Pinus Halepensis
Oak	Walnut	Pinus Maritima
Ash	Poplar	Pinus Insignis
Elm	Willow	Cedar
Sycamore	Cork Oak	

and any other trees that it shall be shown to the satisfaction of the Government are likely to produce good, useful, and valuable timber.

Land to be Fenced.—The proprietor of lands planted as above will be required to erect a sheep and cattle proof fence of post and wire, or a stone wall round the planted land—the same to be kept in thorough repair during the entire term for which trees are to be preserved, as hereinafter mentioned.

No Stock to be Depastured.—The proprietor of any land planted with trees under these regulations will not be allowed to depasture stock thereon to the injury of the young trees.

Period for which Trees must be preserved.—Trees must not be cut down or injured in any way whatever for a period of five years from the date of planting.

Planting on Pastoral Leases.—Pastoral lessees of the Crown wishing to avail themselves of the provisions of clause 27 of this Act, will be required to comply with the above conditions in addition to those contained in that clause.

Upon receipt of a certificate from the Forest Board that a plantation has been formed under the above conditions in any of the Districts to be afterwards referred to, an order will be issued by the Commissioner of Crown Lands in the following form :—

South   [Royal Arms.]   *Australia.*

£ : :   *Order.*   £ : :

No.

It having been duly certified that   acre have been planted with forest trees in accordance with Act No.   of 1878, it is hereby directed that this order shall be available as cash at any Government sale of lands, at auction or otherwise, or in payment of the interest of purchase-money for Crown lands selected on credit, or of any rent due by the holder thereof for the time being, upon condition that this order be exercised within five years from the date hereof.

Given under my hand, at Adelaide, this   day of   18 .

By His Excellency's command,

Commissioner of Crown Lands.

The Act applies only to such portions of the colony as may be declared "Forest Districts" by Proclamation in the *Government Gazette*; and it is clearly stated that its provisions come into operation only from the date of such Proclamation (clause 20).   In order to avoid mistakes and disappointments, it is as well that this should be clearly understood, and that *the Act is not retrospective.*

Following are the districts gazetted to the present time, with the dates when the Act came into force upon them :—

District No. 1—Gazetted November 2nd, 1876 (page 2267).—Comprising portions of the Hundreds of Willunga, Noarlunga, Adelaide, Yatala, Munno Para, Port Adelaide, Barossa, Moorooroo, Belvidere, Kapunda, Waterloo, Alma, Grace, Port Gawler, and the whole of the Hundreds of Nuriootpa, Mudla Wirra, Light, Gilbert, and Saddleworth.

District No. 2—Gazetted November 2nd, 1876.—Comprising the whole of the Hundreds of Wallaroo, Kadina, Tiparra, Clinton, Kulpara, Cameron, Everard, Hall, Upper Wakefield, Stanley, Apoinga, Kooringa, Hanson, Clare, Blyth, Barunga, Boucaut, Hart, Milne, Kingston, Ayers, Andrews, Yackamoorundie, Koolunga, Redhill, Crystal Brook, Narridy, Bundaleer, Reynolds, Anne. All that portion of Yarcowie Agricultural Area, in the Hundred of Terowie, described in the *Government Gazette* of February 22nd, 1872. The whole of the Hundreds of Whyte, Belalie, Yangya, Caltowie, Booyoolie, Napperby, Appila, Tarcowie, Mannanarie, Yongala, Black Rock Plain, Pekina, and Davenport.

District No. 3—Gazetted November 2nd, 1876.—This comprises the whole of the Corporate Town of Strathalbyn ; portion of Districts of Strathalbyn ; portion of the Hundreds of Bremer, Brinkley, Seymour, Coolinong, Malcolm, Bonney, Alexandrina, Nangkita, Goolwa, Encounter Bay; and the whole of the Hundreds of Freeling, Monarto, and Baker.

District No. 4—Gazetted November 2nd, 1876.—Comprising the Hundreds of Robertson, Killanoola, Comaum, Penola, and Monbulla.

District No. 5—Gazetted November 2nd, 1876.—Comprising the whole of the Hundreds of Gambier, Caroline, MacDonnell, Blanche, Kongorong, Benara, Mayurra, Mount Muirhead, and Rivoli Bay.

District No. 6—Gazetted February 1st, 1877 (page 222)—Comprising the whole of the Hundreds of Gregory, Willowie, and Booleroo, in the County of Frome.

CHAPTER IV.

The Commercial Value of Trees as a Crop.

I THINK this is a subject, the full importance of which has not yet
been properly recognised by the public of South Australia. Hitherto
the natural forests of the colony have been sufficient to supply the
ordinary wants of the settlement of the land, and so little a value has
generally been put upon the timber, that, very naturally, trees were
looked upon very much as hindrances to location, which it would be
better were the land free of them. This has always been the case in
newly settled countries, and there has been no exception to the rule
here. Now, however, that the natural forests are gradually disappearing,
and—both from the increased population and larger requirements of the
people generally—the demand for timber is increasing, the true value
of trees as a crop is being realised. Of course, as with every other
commodity, so it is with this one, the demand for it constitutes its
commercial value ; so that it is evident if we can show that trees
are a good marketable article in these days, how much more valuable will
they be ten or fifteen years hence, when our population will be double
what it is now, and our indigenous forest land still further reduced in area.

We have seen in these chapters that the cultivation of trees is necessary to our prosperity as a nation. We require timber for the construction
of our houses, fences, implements, and furniture ; trees are necessary to the
proper regulating of our climate ; they improve our soil and give shelter
to crops and stock ; they are necessary for the supply of those timbers
which we require for the carrying out of our extensive system of railways, jetties, and other grand public works. And besides all these
important requirements of civilised life, trees supply us with fruits, wines,
oils, and other luxuries. Again, what would our landscape be without
them ? We know how bare and dreary-looking some parts of our country
appear, simply from the entire want of trees upon them. In an ornamental
point of view, then, trees are a necessity of our life ; they instruct the
mind in the work of the Creator, and they elevate the soul to things noble
and cultivated. Indeed, as I have remarked in this work, trees have a
wonderfully refining influence about human nature, to such an extent
that by our cultivation of trees, so I think, may our social standard be
estimated.

Now, however, I propose to show, in a very brief manner, how desirable
it is to cultivate trees in these colonies in the light of a *crop* only upon

the land, and purely with reference to the commercial value of the transaction, without reference to any of the other matters just mentioned.

The value of wood as a crop depends of course very much at all times upon local demands, and the situation of the plantation with reference to convenience of carriage to other markets. The larger the population, the more thriving the trade of the district, and the nearer to railway or water carriage, the higher will be the price realised from the sale of timber in proportion. · This is the case all the world over, and the peculiarities of this country form no exception to the rule.

In Britain, trees are now considered by her landed proprietors as one of the most paying of all crops ; and land not otherwise suited for tillage purposes is on all hands being put under the occupation of plantations. It is positively asserted by an authority on forestry in Britain "that land which is from various causes unfit for high farming, will, under wood, at the end of seventy years, under good management, pay the proprietor *nearly three times* the sum of money that he would have received from any other crop upon the same piece of ground."

On land under woods in Europe, with an agricultural value or yearly rental of from 4s. to 10s. per acre, it is quite an ordinary thing to receive from 20s. to 30s. per acre annually from the thinnings of the trees alone ; and when the crop of trees is matured, to receive from £200 to £500 per acre for it. This is of course where the best of management is applied to the crops, and timber of a valuable character is grown upon the sites.

It is true that trees as a crop are longer in being realised than any other crop which may be put upon land; but while they enhance the value of the property for the time being, a much larger amount of money is realised from them in the end.

Now, the question which is of special interest to my readers in connection with this subject is "Does it pay to occupy land with trees in South Australia?" My answer is, undoubtedly it does, and to a much greater extent than it pays in Europe. How I arrive at this conclusion I will now endeavour to show.

Trees come to maturity, or at least to saleable size, in this country in about half the time which it takes the same kinds of trees to arrive at the same stage in Europe ; and as the yearly rent value of land here is much less than at home, we have thus a much less amount of rental to put on the debit side of our plantation accounts. For instance, we will suppose that 100 acres of land are about to be planted in Britain whose agricultural capabilities are worth, say, 15s. per acre of yearly rental. Then, assuming that the trees take 80 years to arrive at maturity, there would thus be a sum of £60 (80 x 15) which would require to be debited to the crop of timber, because this amount could have been got from the land for ordinary agricultural purposes. Then again, in order to arrive at our comparison, we will assume that 100 acres of about the same quality of land are about to be put under a crop of trees in this colony. The rental value of this per acre we will take at 3s. ; and supposing that the trees arrive at maturity here in 40 years, this would give us £6 only as the sum which would have to be deducted from the proceeds of the sale of the timber for the occupation of the land.

By these figures, then, we see that as regards the rental occupancy of the land with trees, the result is greatly in favor of this country as compared with Great Britain.

The expense of formation and management of the plantation is, however, about double in this country to what it is in Britain.

I recently sold the thinnings on ten acres of indigenous forest in one of the forest reserves of the colony, and these realised about £2 per acre over all. The freehold value of the land if sold is not over 20s. per acre! In this case then the *thinnings alone* of the crop realised *double the value of the ground.*

Although the subject is so new in the colony that no statistics can be given of *actual* sales having taken place which could be cited in support of the statement, I am of opinion, which is based upon the present prices of colonial timber, and on the assumption that the trees planted have been of a suitable character to the soil and situation, and that the best of management has been applied to the cultivation and rearing of the trees, that the following may be accepted as a fair estimate of the yield which would result from one acre of plantation in this colony :—

> £2 annually, spread over the first ten years.
> £5 to £8 per acre annually for the next 5 years.
> £10 to £12 per acre annually for the 5 years afterwards.

And probably when the crop is from 25 to 30 years old, it would, as a whole, represent, if cleared and sold in a good market, a value of something like £300 to £400 per acre.

CHAPTER V.

The Effects of Forest Covering upon the Catchment Areas of Reservoirs.

As the storing of water, and the proper arrangement of the surface areas supplying our reservoirs, is a matter of vital importance to the welfare of individuals and well-populated districts in this country, I devote this short chapter to a consideration of how far the planting of trees on the ground from which the water-supply is obtained, affects its supply.

In a country like this, where the annual rainfall is so very uncertain and not evenly distributed over the twelve months of the year, and where, in certain districts of it, the supply of water—it may be for the season—is secured from a few heavy thunderstorms only, it is of the utmost importance that every means should be adopted in order that the catchment areas should be managed in such a way that the loss of this may be reduced to a minimum. As a means to this end I advocate the covering or protecting of the catchment areas with a crop of ligneous growths. Let us, however, look at the subject for a moment, and give the reasons for making this recommendation.

As a rule, the surface areas from which the reservoirs in this country derive their supply of water, consists of hard-baked soil into which any moisture seldom or never penetrates, consequently the reservoirs are dependent entirely upon the surface flow alone for the supply of water to fill them. Hence, two disadvantages arise to the proper management of the reservoirs—first, if a very heavy fall of rain occurs, a large quantity of valuable water is lost by overflowing; and, secondly, the catchment area is washed clean by the heavy fall of rain, and all *debris* and loose soil lying upon it is hurled down with the rush of water: the result being injury to the quality of the water and the gradual silting up of the reservoir. Now, in such a case as this, the covering of the catchment areas with forest growth would diminish the quantity of silt brought down by the heavy falls of rain, and the roots of the trees having rendered the soil open and porous, the surface flow would be retarded at the time, while the reservoirs would be filled more gradually, and the flow into them would continue long after the rains had ceased; hence no loss of water by overflowing would occur.

There is no doubt that large quantities of water are annually lost from the reservoirs of this country by evaporation. This occurs in two ways—first, upon the catchment area, the surface of which, being hot and dry, when the rain falls upon it a considerable proportion of this ascends again in the form of a hot steam, and is of course lost; and, secondly, by hot and dry winds blowing over the surface of the sheet of water in the reservoir a very considerable proportion of water is evaporated. Here, again, the effect of covering the ground with trees would be of great advantage. Speaking of tanks in India of a similar character to our reservoirs, Dr. Brandis (the Inspector-General of Forests for the Government of India) says :—" Now, the effect of clothing the catchment area of these tanks with trees, grass, and brushwood, will certainly be to diminish evaporation, and thus to increase the amount available for the tanks. We may conclude from Mr. Culcheth's experiments that the quantity now lost by evaporation amounts to five-sixths, on an average, of the rain-water that falls upon the catchment area : but with diminished evaporation the flow into the tanks from a wooded area will be much greater than from a bare surface."

Another advantage which would accrue to the reservoirs of this country by the planting of their catchment areas with trees, would be that in summer time many clouds charged with vapour would be attracted by the coolness hovering above the trees, and the result would most probably be a deposit of rain, which would otherwise have passed on had the surface been bare and dry.

I have therefore to recommend that, as a means towards the saving of water, the catchment areas of our reservoirs should be planted with suitable kinds of trees. Even the small spaces of ground devoted to dams by the farmers in the Northern Areas could very judiciously be surrounded and protected by trees, and thus be made serviceable for timber as well as water.

CHAPTER VI.

Some General Remarks on Matters to be Considered Previous to Planting.

PLANTING is an operation upon which too much care and sound practical judgment cannot be brought to bear; and it is as well to understand at the beginning that unless these are applied, the result will not turn out a success.

In the first place, the land to be operated on should be well protected by a proper and secure fence, otherwise animals will get amongst the plants and destroy them. In the second place, a deep and free bed must be provided for the roots of the trees, as if this be not attended to, the plants have not a chance of penetrating their roots down out of the reach of the summer's drought, and hence failures will ensue. In the third place, the character of the land to be operated upon should be well considered, and only such kinds of trees planted as are likely to succeed upon it; and if there are various descriptions of land embraced in the enclosure, trees of sorts adapted to succeed on each description of soil should only be planted. In the fourth place, the plants of each sort used should be of the very best and healthiest description, and no inferior ones planted—as wherever such are used, the crops will be worthless in proportion. In the fifth place, the work of planting the young trees should be carried out on the soundest and safest principles known, as if it be done in a careless and unworkmanlike manner the result will be sure to be unsatisfactory. Bad or unskilled planting is always found out, and even although the plants grow to a certain extent, there is generally an indescribable something about the trees, combined with probably a very sickly appearance, which points to careless or unskilful treatment in the first instance.

To the planter, the season of the year adapted for his operations is one of anxious thought, study, and looking out on every point bearing on the success of his work—at least it ought to be with every one anxious to become a successful planter. Careless or hurried work is always expensive, and only leads to serious loss and great disappointment.

CHAPTER VII.

Table Showing the Number of Trees which can be Planted on an Acre at Stated Distances Apart.

In the following table will be seen at a glance the number of trees it will take to plant an acre of ground with the trees standing at distances from 1ft. to 30ft. plant from plant :—

Distance Apart.	No. of Trees.	Distance Apart.	No. of Trees.
1 foot...............	43,500	12 feet............	302
1½ feet............	19,360	12½ "	270
2 "	10,890	13 "	257
2½ "	6,970	13½ "	239
3 "	4,840	14 "	222
3½ "	3,556	14½ "	207
4 "	2,722	15 "	193
4½ "	2,151	15½ "	181
5 "	1,742	16 "	170
5½ "	1,440	16½ "	164
6 "	1,210	17 "	150
6¼ "	1,031	17½ "	142
7 "	889	18 "	134
7½ "	774	18½ "	127
8 "	680	19 "	120
8½ "	603	19½ "	114
9 "	537	20 "	108
9½ "	482	22 "	90
10 "	435	24 "	75
10½ "	395	26 "	64
11 "	360	28 "	55
11½ "	329	30 "	48

CHAPTER VIII.

—◦◦◦—

Table Showing the Number of Plants Required to Plant Lines
of Trees at Stated Distances Apart.

READY-RECKONING tables are always useful and handy, and I think the
following, showing the number of plants required to plant a mile of a
hedge or avenue of trees, with the plants put in at distances ranging
from 6in. to 100ft. apart, will be of use to my planting friends, and is
therefore deserving of a place in this work :—

Distance Apart.	No. Trees per Mile.	Distance Apart.	No. Trees per Mile.
6 inches	10,560	30 feet	176
1 foot	5,280	31 "	170
2 feet	2,640	32 "	165
3 "	1,760	33 "	160
4 "	1,320	34 "	155
5 "	1,056	35 "	151
6 "	880	36 "	146
7 "	754	37 "	142
8 "	660	38 "	138
9 "	586	39 "	135
10 "	528	40 "	132
11 "	480	41 "	128
12 "	440	42 "	125
13 "	406	43 "	122
14 "	377	44 "	120
15 "	352	45 "	117
16 "	330	46 "	114
17 "	310	47 "	112
18 "	293	48 "	110
19 "	277	49 "	107
20 "	264	50 "	105
21 "	251	55 "	96
22 "	240	60 "	88
23 "	229	65 "	81
24 "	220	70 "	75
25 "	211	75 "	70
26 "	203	80 "	66
27 "	195	85 "	62
28 "	188	90 "	58
29 "	182	100 "	52

C

CHAPTER IX.

Distances Apart at which Forest Trees Should be Planted.

THIS is an important matter, and deserves the best attention of the intending planter. From a careful consideration of the subject before beginning planting, much disappointment will be avoided, and the result, commercially, will be more likely to come up to expectation than if the matter is undertaken without due regard to the peculiarities of soil and situation of the part about to be operated on.

Forest lands, or such parts of a country which we generally find embraced within enclosures devoted to the culture of trees, naturally assume a very varied description, so much so that any one part may, in its physical features, be diametrically opposed to another. Of course this is self-evident, and requires no logical reasoning to show that it is so. Coming, however, to specialities, we may for our purpose define all lands under the following heads, viz., *exposed and high-lying, moderately exposed and at average elevations, and sheltered and low-lying.* Situations such as these embrace pretty nearly every feature of country which will come within the operations of the planter in this colony. I will, therefore, have something to say about each in dealing with the subject in hand.

It is evident that where so much diversity of natural features exists, to plant at one uniform distance apart would be the height of absurdity. Yet that such is often the case in the colony I am aware. The sooner this practice is abandoned and the young plants only put in at such distances one from another in accordance with the special peculiarities of the situation, the better will the result be to the planter and to the country at large.

On exposed and high-lying parts—such as for instance on the bare hill-sides in the Northern Areas, where the elevation ranges from 1,000 to 1,600 ft. above the sea, trees should be planted in such a way that each plant is looked upon as a part of a system in order to the proper protection and shelter of the whole, so that fair growths may be obtained. Trees, in order to succeed well upon any site, must, without exception, have some degree of warmth, and the greater their immunity from disturbing elements so much greater is their chance of success. In high-lying grounds, therefore, such as those to which I have referred, shelter of some sort is absolutely necessary to success in the formation of young plantations, and this can only be most conveniently and cheaply secured by planting the trees thickly on the ground at the beginning.

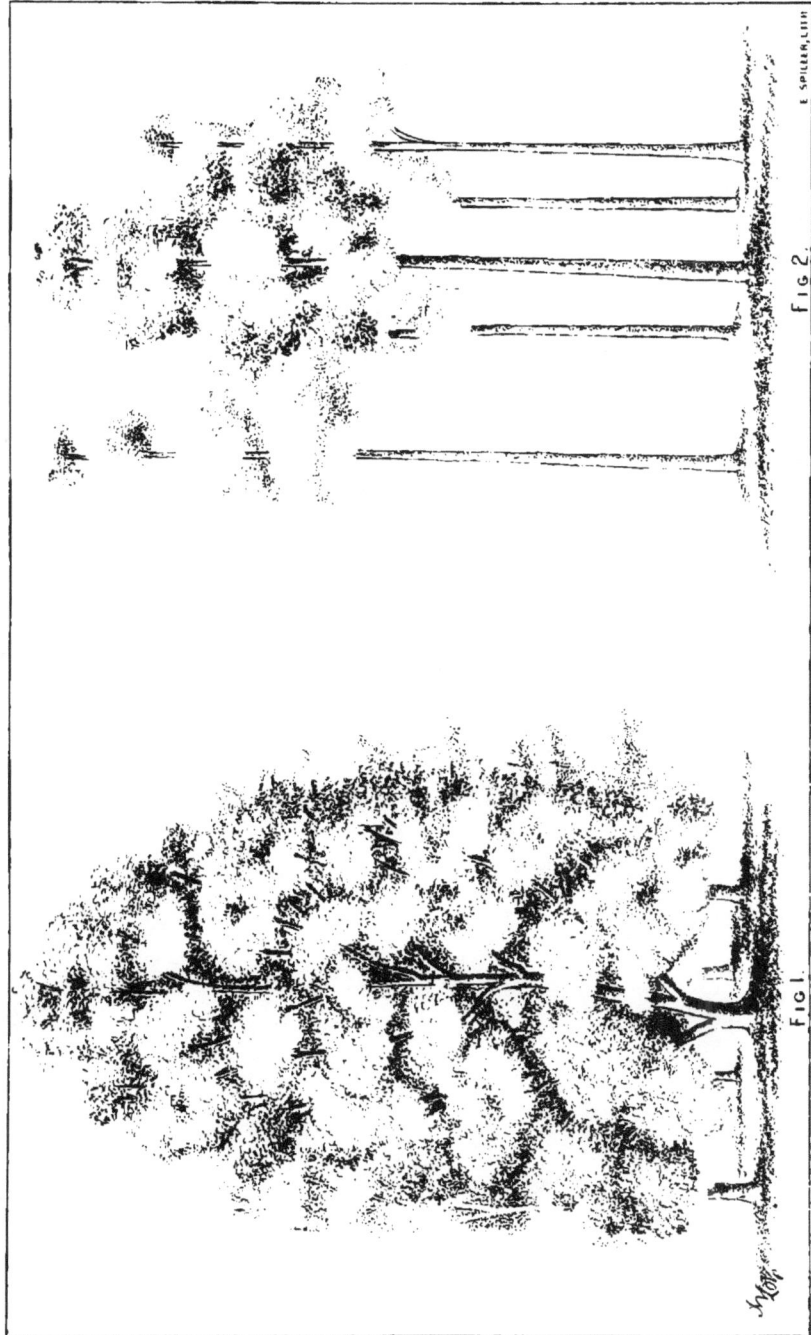

2.

E. SPILLER, LITH

FIG 2.

FIG 1.

They would thus shelter one another at an early age, which would establish a straight growth permanently, and the poorest specimens would be thinned out from time to time as became necessary. On such sites, therefore, I have to advise that the young plants be inserted at about a distance of 5ft. one from another all over the ground forming the plantation.

On such portions of the country which may be classed as *moderately exposed, and lying at average elevations*, the trees should be planted at 6ft. apart in the rows. In such situations also, trees require some artificial shelter for a few years until they have established themselves upon the ground, and this will be secured by planting at the distance named.

The next and last description of country to which I have referred is that of the *low-lying and sheltered* spots. In such situations, it need hardly be remarked, trees grow much more rapidly, and require less attention and care than on the other kinds of country specially mentioned. Taking everything into consideration, therefore, I have to recommend that 8ft. apart is about the proper distance at which young trees should be planted in situations of the kind in this country.

There is a strong inclination amongst the people of this country to plant their trees at wide distances apart—say at from 16ft. to 25ft. In an ornamental point of view, the system is a correct one, but as regards the production of timber, no greater mistake could be made in forestry. By planting at wide distances apart, every encouragement is given to the trees to spread out and develop their branches; consequently a small stunted and gnarled stem is the result when they come to be cut down. Whereas, by planting thickly and thus confining the branches, fine, straight, and superior timber is secured. Fig. 1 represents the form trees assume when planted widely apart; and Fig. 2 their character under the system of close planting.

CHAPTER X.

At what Season of the Year should we Plant.

THIS is another very important matter to be well considered by the intending planter before beginning operations. Much, of course, will depend upon the locality in which the proposed plantation is situated, as to the best time for planting, in consequence of the geographical position of the country giving us early and late seasons, according as our latitude is north or south. Again, the rainy seasons here are so variable, both as to their periods of commencement and duration, that much will depend upon personal local observation at the time as to the best season for planting. Under these circumstances, therefore, it must be understood that the remarks under this head are to be accepted in a general way only, from which, with local observations combined, a fair estimate may always be arrived at by the intelligent planter as to the most suitable time at which to put out his trees.

Of course, it is always an easy matter for those who are planting on a small scale to time their operations in accordance with the condition of the season, and in cases such as this no real risk may be run; but where the operations are upon an extensive scale, planting has frequently to be done at great disadvantages, and often at times when the forester knows that he is working under grave chances of failure in the results. As a rule, however, there will generally be found sufficient seasonable weather for the amount of planting which is likely to be performed by the land-owners of the country.

There is at present considerable difference of opinion as to the proper time for planting in the colony generally—as to whether it should be in autumn or towards spring. Now, there can be no doubt whatever that if the plants are raised with a hardy constitution in the nursery, the sooner they are put out in their permanent sites at the beginning of the rainy season, the more likely are they to establish themselves on the ground beyond injury from the dry weather of summer; but where plants are naturally of a tender nature, thereby necessitating their being reared in houses or under some kind of protection, it would be simple folly to put them out early in winter on cold bleak spots in the plantation. By doing so, would simply mean their destruction by the first blast of cold wind or frost. In this case, then, there is no alternative but to delay planting such kinds of trees until winter is well over, and the frost past for the season. As such kinds are generally grown in pots, no very material check to their vitality will take place in removal, consequently their growth will, in the generality of cases, go on, and the young tender shoots of the fibres will have sufficient time to penetrate into the soil before the last rains for the season are over. I find that, with very few exceptions, the *Eucalypti* are unable to withstand the effects of the early and most severe frosts, and that if they are planted out too soon a considerable percentage is lost before the winter is over. Under these circumstances, I have to advise that trees of this kind be not transplanted out into the plantations until the worst of the cold weather is over for the season.

In the case of trees of a hardy constitution, however, and which have therefore been raised without much regard to protection, these may be transplanted out into the plantation any time between the first of June and end of August.

All the hardier kinds of *Coniferæ* should be put out immediately after the first good rains, in order that they may get the full benefit of the season's growth, which follows shortly after this takes place. The earlier autumn planting is performed the more successful it will be.

Deciduous trees may be transplanted out as soon as they have ripened their young shoots, which stage is indicated by the leaves becoming dry and losing their green color.

In early seasons, pines and deciduous trees may be planted out in the month of May.

CHAPTER XI.

How the Ground should be Prepared before Trees are Planted upon it.

In moist climates, such as those of Europe and North America, the preparation of ground previous to planting being done upon it is generally considered of secondary moment to other matters connected with forestry; but in this country, where the climate is such as to demand that every possible means be availed of in order to secure a supply of moisture to the plants during the driest period of the year, this is a subject of the first importance, and upon the due consideration of which will depend the success, or otherwise, of the operations. I shall therefore devote a short chapter to a few hints on the subject.

In the preparation of ground for planting, we must always keep in view to do so in such a way that its capacity for absorbing and retaining moisture will be increased, at the same time that the surface herbage upon it will be decreased to such an extent that the destruction of the trees upon it by fire will be entirely avoided, or at least reduced to a minimum. These are the chief matters for our consideration under this heading; the question then at once arises, how are these to be secured? The answer is, by thorough cultivation only. By cultivation we secure a bare surface, free from grass; the soil is loosened to such a depth that the tender and delicate rootlets of the trees can penetrate beyond the reach of climatic excesses; the soil, in this case, takes the place of a sponge, which absorbs the rain as it falls, and carries down with it a store of organic and inorganic food for the roots, besides acting as a reservoir for the water which would otherwise have run away to waste; the hot rain penetrating down into the ground adds warmth and life to what would otherwise, in all probability, have been a cold ungenial site; while, again, where there is thorough cultivation there is generally entire freedom from frosts and stagnant water.

The ground intended to be planted, if it has not been under cultivation previously, should be systematically ploughed to a depth of not less than six inches before the end of the winter rains, and afterwards the land should be rigidly summer-fallowed by ploughing and harrowing several times during the summer months, so that by the next rainy season the surface herbage upon the site shall have been thoroughly rotted and killed out. Immediately after the first good rains of the year following the first ploughing, the ground should be re-ploughed, and at the same time subsoiled to a depth of at least fifteen inches, or more if possible, after which it will be in good condition for the reception of the young plants.

In the case of planting on land which has undergone a preparation by means of the plough and subsoiler, the usual method is simply that of opening holes in it, at the desired distance apart, of size sufficient for the reception of the young trees, as the work of planting them proceeds. In this case the land is clean, free, and open to a depth of over fifteen inches, and therefore it is, in all respects, in a fit condition to admit the roots of the young trees getting down into it. For all small plants, it is not absolutely necessary to further open the subsoil where the ground has been so prepared; but for large plants some further opening up of this will be required when the holes are dug. This should be done to at least a depth of 18in., and the holes made 18in. to 2ft. wide on top. Land which has been properly ploughed and subsoiled ought, if the work has been properly done, to be in the very best condition for planting, and this with holes as above is in a much better state for the reception of large young trees than land prepared with holes 4ft. square and no ploughing.

Without dilating further upon this subject, I would simply give my readers this piece of advice :—That while taking care *never* to dig the holes *less* than 18in. square, make them much larger if you can, as by so doing the better will it be for the plants in the end.

By deep subsoiling, the roots of the plants get well down the first season, and moisture will be drawn up to them by the heat of the sun, and perfect success will be the result.

. In planting on hills and mountain slopes, where no cultivation can well be brought to bear on the land as a preparation for planting, holes should be opened on the natural surface all over the part to be put under trees, and at the distance apart that may be considered proper, according to the nature of the case and the object in view. These holes should be made of sizes according to the nature of the land : that is, if the land is naturally deep and porous, they should be dug about 24in. on the side of the square on top, and of the same depth; but if it be retentive in the subsoil, the holes should be made 30in. square on top and 24in. deep. By this method of planting, I have been very successful in growing extensive plantations in uncultivated districts. Should the soil be of a hard clayey nature, the holes had better be opened a month or two before planting, in order that by the action of the sun and weather it may become pulverised and sweetened before being put round the tender rootlets of the plants.

In all cases, the soil taken from the bottom of the holes should be returned there, and the surface portion reserved to be put about the roots of the young trees when planting them.

CHAPTER XII.

~~∽◦✠◦∽~~

How Young Trees should be Planted.

Of all the varied operations of the arboriculturist, I know of none upon which the success of his labors depend so much as that of careful planting. That three-fourths of the failures which we are always hearing about are entirely due to this operation being done in a careless and unworkmanlike manner, there is no reason to doubt. While I cannot, therefore, impress too strongly upon my readers the absolute necessity there is at all times for careful and skilled supervision of this work, I will now endeavor to give some hints here as to how it should be done.

Before planting begins, the site should be carefully inspected in all its different parts and a decision come to as to what particular kinds of trees are likely to succeed best upon it. It will sometimes be found that in an enclosure of even five or ten acres, there exists such a marked difference of soil and subsoil in places that the ground will have to be taken up in sections, and each one planted without reference to the other.

One great source of failure in planting is, careless and quite unnecessary exposure of the roots of the young trees during their translation from the nursery to their sites in the plantation. I refer in this remark both to cases where the trees are reared by the planter himself, and to plants which are purchased from nurserymen and conveyed some distance to the scene of action, Let me give one or two cautions with reference to this matter.

Should you purchase plants from a nursery, see that they are *very carefully* packed and their roots covered with *damp* straw or other substance before they leave the establishment. This remark has reference more particularly to deciduous trees which are grown openly in the nursery ground. Plants in pots should be carefully packed in boxes with damp moss round them to prevent breakage, and at the same time, in order to keep the plants moist. As a rule, however, customers may depend upon nurserymen packing the plants well, as it is to their interest to see that they arrive in good condition and give a good return.

Much of the damage to young plants occurs, however, *after* they have left the hands of the nurseryman. They are taken home and probably are allowed to lie about in bundles without watering, &c., for several days until a convenient time arrives to plant them. I know of a case in the north where plants were allowed to lie in the verandah for a fort-night, with their roots all exposed, and then planted. The result, of course, was *nil*.

As soon as purchased plants arrive home, have them *sheughed*, or laid in a nice cool and moist spot in the garden or plantation. If they are in bundles, undo them, and spread the plants out singly, and carefully cover all the roots with well-pulverised soil. Should the weather be dry, give a good watering. Plants in pots may be kept in the boxes, and kept moist until they are required.

Where the plants are grown by the planter himself, there is less risk of danger from exposure, as they can be lifted and taken to the planta-tion in such numbers and at such times only as may be found most conve-nient. Under such circumstances, it is best and safest to lift in the morning, and take out to the plantation only as many as may be required for that day's planting. On arrival at plantation, the deciduous trees should be laid in the ground, and the plants in pots kept in the boxes, and taken out as they are required.

A good plan with trees which are grown in the open ground is, to dip their roots in a *puddle* of earth-and-water immediately they are lifted. This prevents the air taking an injurious effect upon the small and tender *spongioles* of the rootlets, and I have, therefore, strongly to recommend its general adoption in this country. I shall refer to this operation afterwards in these pages as that of *puddling*.

I now come to advise as to how the trees should be planted. In doing this, it will be necessary to refer to open-root plants, plants in bamboo tubes, plants in pots, and sowing the seed in the plantation, each separately.

In planting, it is always necessary for two persons to be at the operation —say a man and a lad; the lad to hold the plant, and the man to fill in the soil and see to the roots. It is, of course, understood that the holes have been already opened in accordance with the directions given.

First, then, in regard to the planting of trees which have been grown in the open ground in the nursery. It is understood that these are, as a rule, strong plants, and that they have been raised with all their roots attached. Should the hole be too deep for the plant, fill in some of the good soft mould which will generally be found on the surface of the ground. When of the required depth, the boy will then hold the plant erect in the centre of the hole, while the man spreads out the roots and fibres of the plant with his hands and fills in the top mould which had been removed from the hole. Should there be *layers* of roots, it will be necessary to cover them up separately, beginning, of course, with the lowest and taking the others in rotation. In Fig. 3 I show a young tree, with four layers of roots, being planted, and at that stage when the hole is half-filled up. While the lowest tier is being covered with the soil, the others should be held carefully up with the hand and only released as the soil comes up to their levels. As this operation goes on, the boy should move the plant gently up and down, so as to settle the soil about the roots, but this should be discontinued when about a third of the hole is filled in and the soil feels heavy upon the roots. After the soil is filled in to the top, it should then be firmly pressed down with the feet, and the indentation thus made afterwards filled up with loose soil, and left without further tramping down.

Never press down the soil upon the roots of the plants *until the hole is full*, as the looser and freer it is about the tender fibres, the sooner will they strike into it in their new position, and become established once more.

As a rule, transplanted trees should stand a *little* deeper in the soil (say from ½ to 1 inch according to size of plant) in the plantation than they stood in the nursery lines.

Be careful to see that the best soil is always put round the roots of the trees. This will ensure a much better result than if the soil is put in the hole indiscriminately without reference to its quality or fineness.

When the insertion is completed, the plant should stand as represented in Fig. 4; that is, with all the roots well below the surface of the ground and the ground slightly sloping from the outside to the stem of the tree. I cannot condemn in too severe terms a system of planting trees which I often see carried out in the colony: that is, of planting the tree on a *raised mound*. This does not give them a chance to live throughout the summer, and I am convinced that considerable losses have been sustained from the system hitherto.

The plants grown in *bamboo* tubes are more easily and much more cheaply planted than those grown in any other way. Two smart men will put in about 500 plants by this system in a day. As elsewhere explained, however, it can only, so far as I have yet seen, be used in the rearing of the *Eucalypti ;* hence its application to general forestry is somewhat limited.

The tubes should be conveyed from the nursery to the plantation in boxes about 18in. square on top, and 9in. deep, with handles of wire as shewn in Fig. 72. Boxes this size will hold over 200 tubes, or about as many as will last a couple of planters one-half of a day. Fig. 77 represents a box full of plants, and ready for the planter to begin work with. A box should be provided for each set of two men planting in one row, and there should be two full sets of boxes, so that, while the men are planting with the one set in the forenoon, a man may be filling the other with the tubes in the nursery, and have these brought out to the plantation by noon, and thus the emptying and filling will go on regularly without loss of time.

Two men are necessary to each row, one with a spade, and the other with the box of plants. It is, of course, presumed that the ground has been previously thoroughly ploughed and subsoiled. On such lands, the plants in bamboos can be planted very easily. The man with the spade digs up and moulders down the soil for a space of about 12in. all round, and as deep as the spade will go, on the spot where the tree is to be inserted. This done, he will then sink his spade into this prepared spot, in a perpendicular manner, and cut out a space for the tube. The man with the box of plants, will now take a plant in one hand and a trowel (Fig. 73) in the other, and placing the tube against the cut edge of the

3.

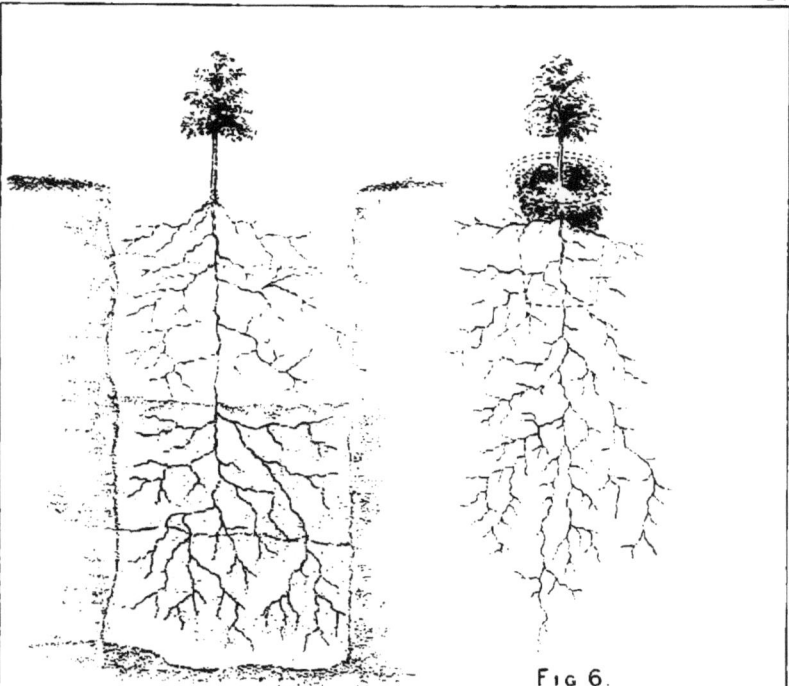

FIG 3.

FIG 6.

FIG 4

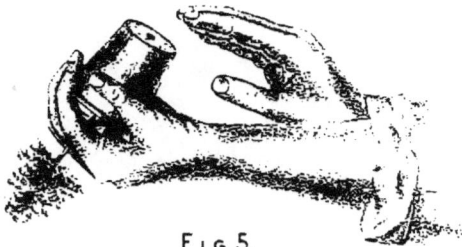

FIG 5.

E SPILLER LITH

hole prepared, put fine well-pulverised soil round it, pressing this gently down once or twice, as he puts the soil in the hole. As a rule, it will be found that a trowel answers all practical purposes, and while one man is planting the tree, the other can be preparing the next hole, and so the work goes on smoothly and without waste of time.

Care must always be taken to sink the top of the bamboo about an inch or so *below* the surface of the ground, and to gently press the soil above its top, and round the stem of the young tree. Where the planting is extensive, and proper protection cannot be given to the young plants, a couple of turfs, or a plough furrow should be thrown up about a foot from the plants, on the side towards the prevailing winds. These different points are shewn in Figs. 75 and 76, to which reference is directed.

If the tubes are properly prepared before being used, they can be planted whole as they come from the nursery beds; but if they have not been so treated, and the wood is hard and tough, it is as well to gently split them on one side before they are planted out. This can be done by the man just as they are about to be put in the ground.

I now come to describe the operation of planting trees which have been reared in pots.

The plants should be conveyed to the plantation in the pots, and distributed at the holes as they are required. The ground having been prepared as already directed, and the holes opened, the work of planting may now proceed. One man attends to the plant, and the other stands by with a spade ready to put the soil into the hole as it is required by the other. In removing the plant from the pot, this should be done by spreading the left hand over the top of the pot, with the stem of the plant between the two middle fingers, and with the right hand grasping the bottom of the pot, turning it upside down, and then gently striking its edge upon the handle of the spade, or by tapping the bottom with the other hand, as shown in Fig. 5. The plant will now come out with the earth and roots in a solid mass. The planter will then gently agitate and knock off all the soil about the roots with the exception of about an inch or so at the top, which must be kept intact, and the liberated roots should now be unwound from their circular or spiral form to their full length, all as shown in Fig. 6. The tree is now ready to be planted. This operation must be carefully done, and may be described as follows:—Getting down upon his knees, the planter, holding the plant carefully in his left hand, with the right one will place the end of the taproot of the plant *at the bottom* of the hole, and then, getting soil from the man with the spade, will pack it loosely round the roots, spreading these out to their full length, and taking up each layer carefully as he comes to it, all as described for such operations in connection with open-root planting. This is work which cannot be done hurriedly, as every care must be taken to avoid breaking any of the fine fibrous roots with which a plant of this kind is generally well supplied.

Regarding the sowing of the tree seeds in the plantations on the sites which the plants are intended to occupy, a few remarks will suffice. The ground all ploughed and subsoiled, as advised, spaces should be prepared by digging and smoothing down the soil to about 12in. to 18in. square on top, for the reception of the seeds.   The soil on these spaces should be made nice and fine, so that there may be a good bed for the seed.   These places made ready, a man, provided with a small bag containing the seed, should go along each row, and bending down at each spot, remove a little of the soil with his hand, and then placing a few seeds on the place, cover it up again to a depth of from ½in. to 1in., according to the size and nature of the seed which is being sown at the time.   If three or four seeds are used, keep them an inch or two apart.   Should all germinate, they can be thinned out to one plant after it is seen which is likely to become the best tree in every respect.   This sowing of the seeds should be done as early as possible after the winter rains have set in.   Care should be taken to use fresh seed only, in order that no blanks may occur, and the spots sown ought to be slightly under the general surface of the ground, though not in such a hollow as will allow the lodgment of water.   Seed-sowing may be done at from 4 to 5ft. apart, as blanks are likely to occur, and if at all successful, this will prevent the necessity of much filling-up in after years.

All planting should be performed in such a way that the trees will stand alternately in the rows ; that is, the trees of the second row should be placed about midway between every two trees of the first row, and those of the third row in the middle of the second, and so on throughout the whole plantation.   I show this in Fig. 7.

In the majority of cases—that is where not more than from fifty to one hundred acres are about to be planted in one season, the planting should only be done in weather really suited for the purpose.   Never plant out trees on a hot day, but when the weather is cloudy or somewhat dampish push on the work as much as possible.   Trees planted on a dull day are almost sure to give a good result, but if they are put out in sunny, warm weather, disastrous consequences are sure to follow.

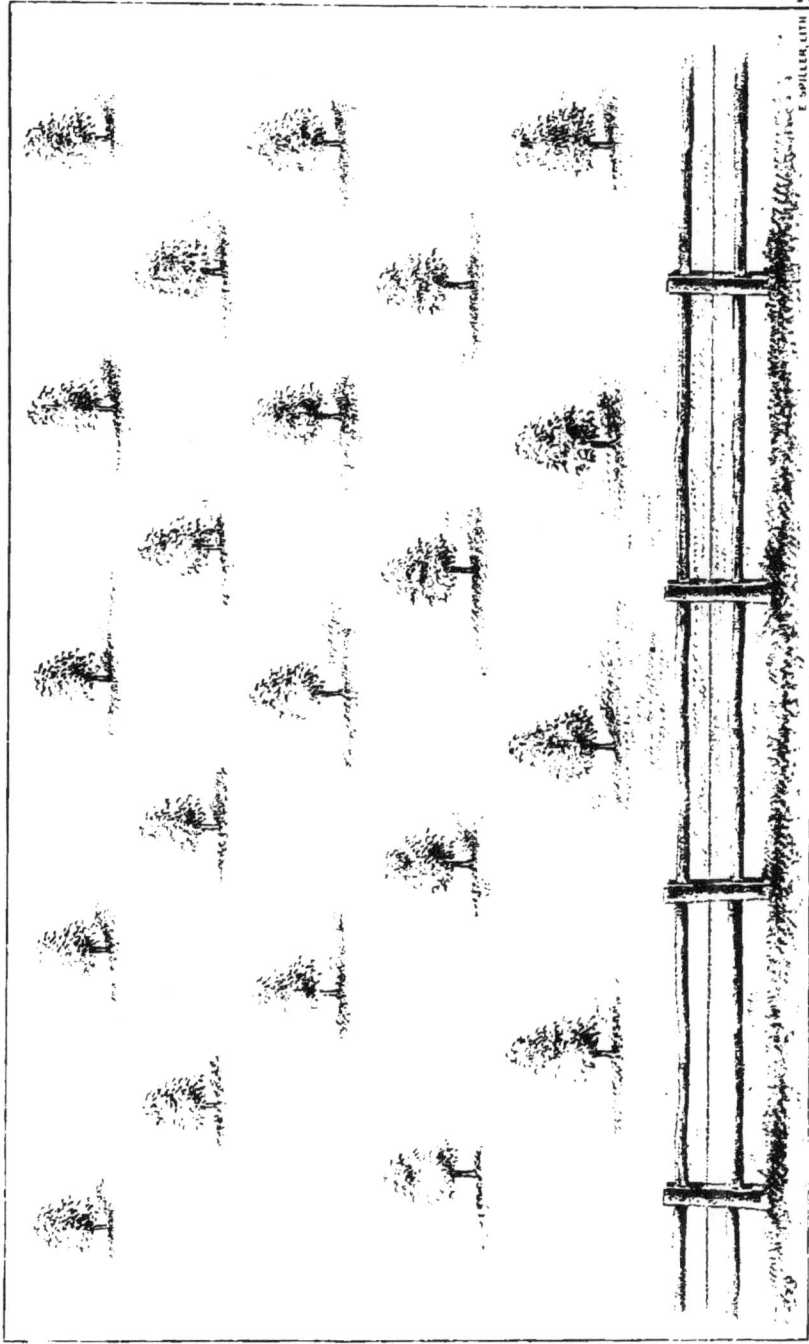

FIG 7.

E. SPILLER, LITH

CHAPTER XIII.

Treatment of Young Trees after Planting.

In cold and moist climates, young trees do not require much attention to be paid to them after planting. Here, however, where the climate is dry and uncertain, the reverse is the case; and upon their proper care or neglect after being put out into the plantation, so will the result be success or failure. It matters not how carefully the trees may have been reared and planted, if they are not attended to judiciously afterwards, the plantation is sure to be unsatisfactory. I think a much better result would be obtained from planting inferior plants and putting them under good management afterwards, than would flow from the planting of good trees and letting them alone as soon as they were put out.

The subject which we are about to consider is one of which, unfortunately, the most of planters in this country do not seem to recognise its importance. I have frequently seen fine young plantations ruined from pure neglect and want of attention after their formation. It is to be hoped, therefore, that these lines will tend to a better state of things in this respect in the colony. I now proceed to give some general directions in this matter.

It will sometimes be found that the plants grown in pots are of such a spindley character, that they cannot support themselves. This, unfortunately, is frequently the case, as they are "drawn up" by being kept too long under cover. As I already said, avoid plants of this character as much as possible, but it will of course sometimes happen that plants of the kind will be used. In this case, it is necessary that they be properly staked for the first few years after planting, until they have established themselves in their sites. It takes a long time for trees which have been drawn up to recover themselves properly and again become shapely and strong plants. Indeed, I question very much if they ever sufficiently recover themselves to make good trees. Plants of this character should certainly *never* be used for ornamental purposes.

Should the weather be dry at the time of planting, it will give the young plants a good chance to recover the effects of removal and strike their roots into the soil of their new site, if a good soaking of water be given to them immediately after they are planted. Of course this can only be done where a few hundreds of trees are planted; as the operation, although beneficial, could not—on the score of expense—be applied to plantations containing from ten to thirty thousand trees. Artificial watering in this way, should only be resorted to when the weather is extremely dry and there are no signs of immediate rains. Loosen the soil round the plants the day after watering.

In about ten days or a fortnight after trees have been planted, the soil about them should be nicely hoed for a space of at least 2ft. all round, and this should be repeated from time to time during the season, as the ground shows signs of baking or becomes overgrown with weeds. A good time to execute hoeing of this kind is after a shower of rain, when the soil will work freely and pulverise nicely under the hoe. This hoeing should be done in the driest of weather, as the loose soil will draw moisture from the air to the roots of the plants. I hardly know of any operation which conduces more to the success of young plants than this one.

I have already casually referred to the providing of some sort of protection to young trees for the first year after they are put out into the plantation. Good results will unquestionably flow from this, and it should be resorted to if it can be done conveniently and without a great deal of expense. Strong deciduous trees do not require protection of this kind, but Gums, Pines, Sterculias, Lagunarias, Moreton Bay Figs, Araucarias, and Cedars, &c., will be much benefited by it. For this purpose use whatever may be easiest procured, such as old palings, posts, old bags, &c., If good strong palings are sawn up for the purpose, they can be made available for several successive plantations, as it is not necessary to continue protecting the plants after the end of the summer succeeding the year of planting.

Owing to the extremely dry weather experienced here in summer time, it is necessary that the ground round the sites of all small and tender plants should be thoroughly " mulched." This operation should be performed about the end of the rainy season, and immediately before the hot weather sets in. This may be either in September or October, and perhaps even later, and its performance must of course be guided altogether by the character of the season at the time. It is best done after a shower of rain. As the operation is not generlly understood, I will now give a short description as to how it should be performed :—

Hoe and thoroughly loosen the soil for a space of 3ft. round the tree ; then prepare the mulch, which should consist of short well-dried grass, road sweepings—or, what is perhaps better than anything else, well-rotted and thoroughly-dried stable manure, with lots of short straw mixed with it. Take this " mulch " and lay it all over the hoed ground to a depth of at least nine inches, packing it solid and taking care not to press it too closely about the plant, but to leave room for a free current of air to pass round its stem.

This done, soil should be spread round the edge of the mulch, and a little spread over its top, in order to prevent its removal by the winds.

With this covering the soil underneath will remain damp during the most drying period of summer. The operation, as completed, is represented in Fig. 4. The mulch should not be removed until the hot weather is over and the winter rains have begun again.

One thing must be guarded against, and that is, never to mulch with green grass or wet manure, as if this be done, and frequent rains come afterwards, the plants are sure to die from heating or over-richness as the case may be.

If planters will look after their plantations in the manner indicated in this chapter, good results are sure to follow their work.

CHAPTER XIV.

General Planting on Farms.

THE chief objects in planting on arable farms are, to secure shelter for the fields in them and a supply of timber for the use of their proprietors, and also to enhance the general value of the holdings.

In planting on such farms as are generally found in South Australia, the enclosures are most advantageously laid out in the form of belts, with their sides extending at right angles to the prevailing winds of the district. In laying out such belts, it is always advantageous to enclose with each of them any lateral height that may project from the main body into the adjoining fields, just so far as may be considered necessary in order to break the straight line, and at the same time secure a degree of shelter to live stock from winds that may blow from the points in line with the main belt. Another point to attend to in laying off such plantations as I am now referring to is, that the greatest extent should be kept, as far as possible, along the higher-lying portion of the land; as it is evident that a plantation on a high part of a farm produces more shelter to the surrounding fields than one situated on a low-lying part. My remarks on this point will be more readily understood by reference to Fig. 8, which shows a high-lying farm of 1,000 acres, properly planted. If there be any gravelly, sandy, or poor knoll or ridge of land on the farm, it should also, if possible, be planted in order both to produce shelter and have ornamental effect; and this should be done irrespective of the belts laid out for the express purpose of sheltering the lands of the farm, as such poor spots are in all cases more remunerative, ultimately, under trees than were they kept under the plough; and, besides, when planted, they give such a clothed look to the farm as to enhance its value very much in the estimation of persons of refined taste; and this often goes far in securing a high price for land.

In planting, the proprietor should, in all cases, use only the sorts of trees that are likely to succeed well on his land, while at the same time he should have an eye to the future value of the crop in respect to its becoming useful for his own immediate purposes and to its market value as a return from his land.

As to the proportion of land that should properly be put under trees on an ordinary arable farm, I should say that at least ten acres in every hundred should be occupied by them. And besides this extent of plantation on each farm, there should be several small groups of trees distributed on well-chosen points in the fields, and also

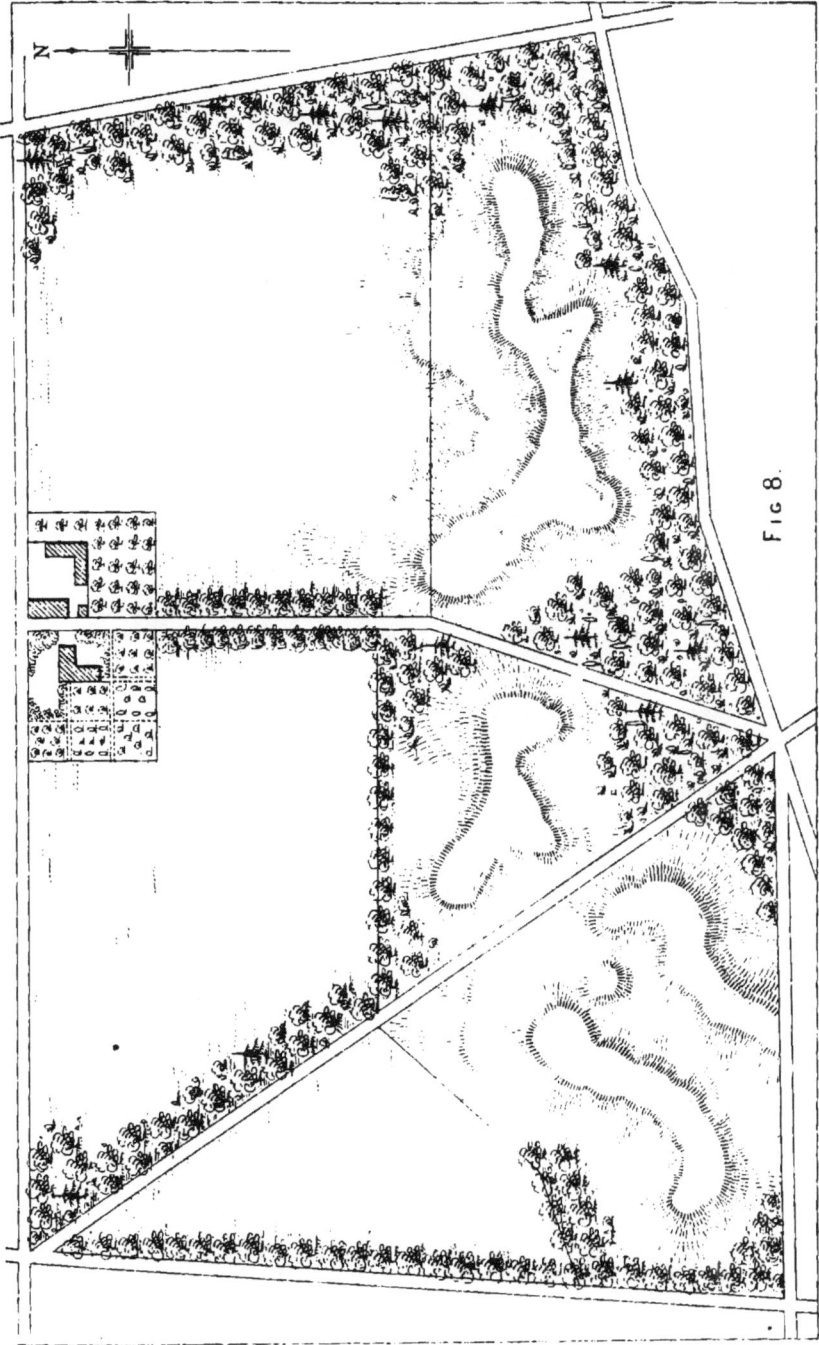

Fig 8.

several rows of trees on the fence lines ; all so as to secure the requisite conditions for a sufficiency of moisture over the country, to maintain a supply of timber for the farm, to produce the degree of shade and shelter necessary for the healthy growth of crops and development of live stock, and to give each and every subject that pleasing and ornamental aspect which at the present time is so much wanted and sought after.

The larger the piece of ground devoted to a plantation, the better will the trees succeed as a whole. Be advised, therefore, to plant as much as possible in large masses.

CHAPTER XV.

―――⟐――

The Fencing of Plantations.

THAT all lands devoted to the rearing of young trees must be thoroughly and securely fenced is, perhaps, hardly necessary to remark here, but the subject being a component part of the forester's duties, I devote a short chapter to its consideration.

While the trees are in a young and tender condition they are very liable to injury from the trampling and browsing of herbivorous animals, consequently it is absolutely necessary to protect them while they are in this state, if successful planting is looked for. Independent, however, of protection from stock which trees derive from the ground they occupy being thoroughly enclosed, there is another advantage which is secured to the young crop from the fence, and that is *shelter* to a more or less extent, according to the character of the material used. It has been frequently remarked by those engaged in the formation of plantations, that a very slight shelter from cold or hot winds, by the boundary fence breaking these, has a wonderful effect upon the growth of the young trees inside, to such an extent that those trees nearest the fence are generally so much healthier and stronger than the others as to have the appearance of being some years older. The effect and advantage, then, of this is that the outer rows of trees get up quickly, and tend to protect those further in the body of the plantation. As a rule, it is found that well-fenced plantations in Europe are from eight to ten years in advance of those which are badly or not at all fenced.

It may be remarked here that young plantations in this country do not, generally speaking, require the protection of fences after they have attained the age of six to ten years, according to the character of the trees constituting them, as at this stage the trees should, under fair management, be sufficiently grown to enable them to stand good against the inroads of stock.

Recognising, then, the immense value of good and judicious fences to the welfare of the young trees in our plantations when in their early stage of growth, it is of paramount importance for those about to plant, to enclose the ground intended to be operated on with a fence of such a character as will give this shelter.

It is evident that much will depend upon the local supply of certain materials—whether it be great or small—as to the kind of fence to be erected round a plantation. This, no doubt, is the proper rule to be guided by in a matter of the kind. In enclosing a very large district for planting, and where this is done for utility only without much consideration in an ornamental point of view, the fence need not be all of one description, but may be made of various materials, as may be found most convenient and least expensive. For instance, it may be constructed of stone alone where this material is abundant on a certain part of the line; with wood alone in another part where stone is not so convenient; with posts and wire on a third part of the line where this would be cheapest and perfectly serviceable, and so on.

CHAPTER XVI.

Planting Trees Along Fences and Roads.

FENCE-ROW trees, if planted properly and rightly managed afterwards, are of great importance to the farming community and to all agricultural areas generally. This would especially be the case in this country, where there are extensive tracts of land under cultivation without the sign of a tree upon them. As yet almost nothing has been attempted in this way by our farmers, but I think it is safe to assert that, ere long, the time will come when its importance will be recognised, and the system of planting rows of trees along the fences will become general.

I have strongly to recommend the landowners of the colony to plant trees in this way for the following reasons, namely :—1st, by this means shelter and shade are given to stock and crops whereby larger returns will be procured ; and 2nd, the result being a finely-clothed and ornamental appearance to the farm, an enhanced value of property will be secured to a very considerable extent. These objects can be obtained without any injury whatever being done to the agricultural produce of the farm.

In planting trees in the manner stated, the plants may be put in one or more rows, as may be considered necessary in accordance with the requirements of the particular line being operated on, by its situation in respect to general and local winds. Thus, where the line faces the north or north-west it would be advisable to plant several rows of trees together, in order to afford more protection to the crops and stock in the fields to leeward of it. A single or even double row of trees in this case would not be nearly sufficient to give the desired shelter from the winds.

As a rule, one row of trees is not sufficient in our northern areas to give shelter, nor would the trees be likely under such circumstances to attain to any considerable degree of size or beauty. In this country it may almost be put down as a *sine qua non* in planting operations of whatsoever kind they may be, that the trees must be planted in considerable bodies together, in order that, by their mutually sheltering and protecting one another, they may grow healthily and of a strong and robust habit. If done otherwise, the result will, in the generality of cases, be found unsatisfactory.

Of course there are cases where a single row would be quite sufficient, such as in some sheltered spot with a good quiet aspect, but such spots are the exception here.

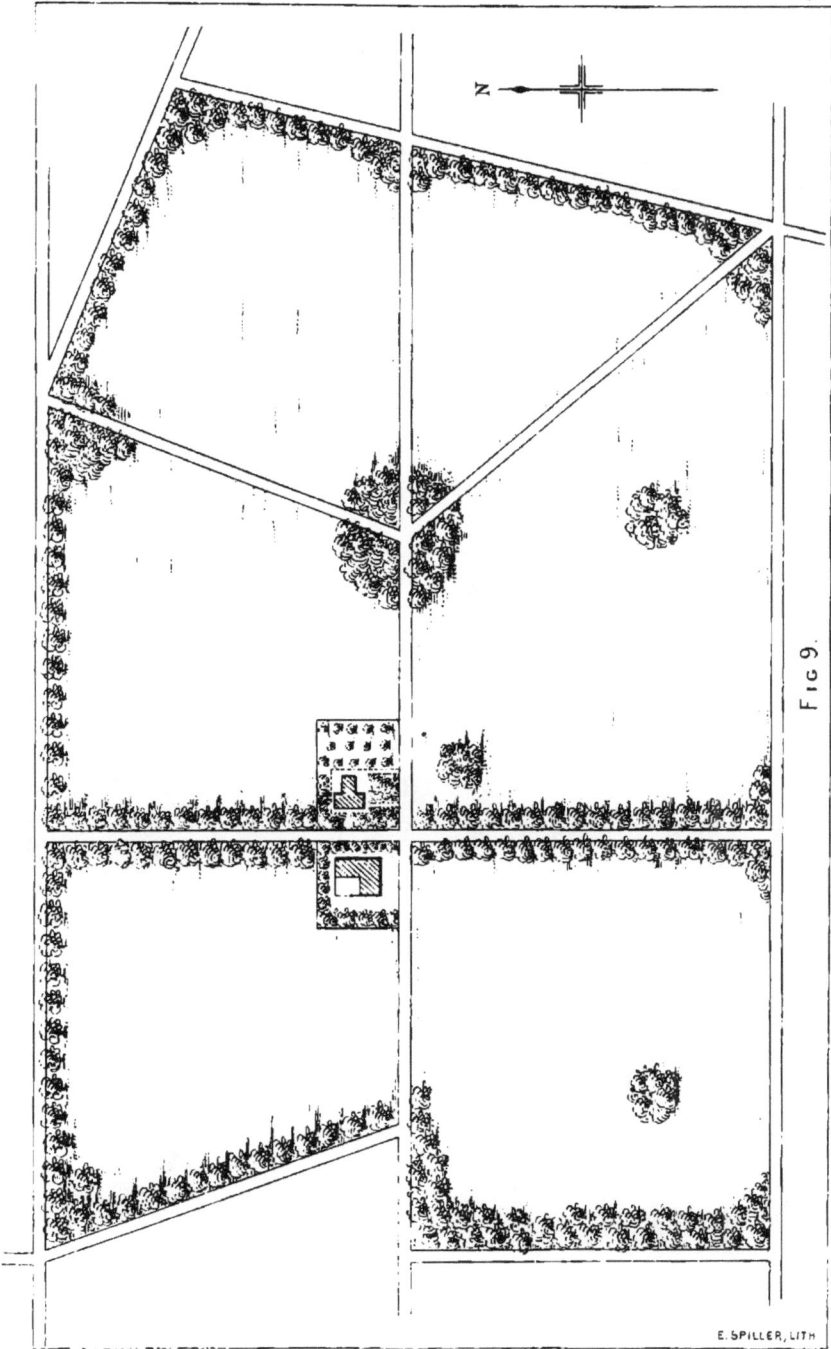

Fıɡ 9.

E. SPILLER, LITH.

I would advise, therefore, that in planting belts of trees in the manner referred to, not less than four rows of trees be made to constitute the plantation, but more if deemed advisable, all in accordance with the character of the situation being operated on. The trees should, under all circumstances, be planted alternately in the rows, so that when they attain a fair size, a person looking at the plantation in any direction cannot, if the trees have succeeded to expectation, see the fields beyond. This is very important where the object in forming plantations is purely to obtain shelter from prevailing winds.

In Fig. 9 I give sketch of a low-lying farm of 1,000 acres, showing plantations and rows of trees along the fences and roads.

In selecting trees for planting in belts or rows for shade and shelter, it should always be borne in mind to choose such only as are of a spreading and densely-foliaged nature. Trees of an upright habit—such as the Lombardy Poplar and Upright Cypress—are, unless planted very thickly upon the ground, far from being desirable for this purpose. Much, of course, will depend upon the soil, aspect, and general natural features of the ground as to the particular kinds of trees which should be planted, and care should at all times be taken to plant such only as may be safely relied upon to do well upon the site.

As trees put out in this manner have little or no shelter, and are therefore apt to become injured by the winds, I have to advise that they be planted pretty thickly upon the ground, so that they may give one another shelter. The best way to do this is to plant the trees which are to remain on the ground as the permanent crop, at about 24ft. apart, and to fill up all the spaces between them with other kinds, which should be removed as thinnings from time to time as may become necessary. Wattles may very judiciously be used in this way as the *nurses*. Care will have, however, to be taken to avoid allowing these nurses to encroach too much upon the standards, as this would spoil their spreading habit, and therefore make them unfit for the purpose for which they were planted. Keep the nurses well together, but do not let them touch those trees which they are meant to protect.

Cultivate the ground as deeply as possible before planting, and keep the soil free and open about the standards for a good distance round their roots. If this be done for a few years, the trees will grow rapidly, and soon give excellent shelter to the lands around them.

Do not attempt to prune trees which are required to form shelter of this kind, but rather encourage them to assume their characteristic habits, and spread out their branches as much as possible.

CHAPTER XVII.

Planting on the Sea-coast.

THERE is no doubt that planting on the sea-coast is a work of very great difficulty, and consequently it is often attended with many disappointments when undertaken. This is especially the case in this climate, where, besides the usual drawback of the situation to contend with, there is the no less difficult one of the extreme dry weather in summer to be considered. However, by care, attention, and some nursing during the first two or three years of the plantation's existence, a fair result may at all times be looked for.

Of course, it must always be understood that in planting near the sea, it is seldom indeed that the result will ever be good timber trees. Ligneous growths, as a rule, are very shy of the blasting influences of the sea breezes, and we invariably find that even those kinds of trees which grow in such sites are liable to become somewhat stunted, and show a tendency to a crouching habit, as if they shrunk from and tried to throw off the cold and withering winds charged with saline matter. This dislike of trees to the sea-coast is quite apparent from the fact that we find the greater extent of sea-coast barren, and generally devoid of these.

The grand object in seaside planting is to secure shelter either to houses, stock, or crops. Many places on the coast which would otherwise be uninhabitable from their exposure to the sea-breeze, have been converted into pleasant and beautiful abodes by careful and well-executed planting. To do this, however, requires a greater amount of skill and practical oversight than planting trees under any other condition which will come within the planter's experience. Little assistance will be derived from nature, so that the best of artificial means must be applied to the subject in order to arrive at the object aimed at.

As a rule, also, it will be found that planting on the sea-coast is considerably more expensive work than the operation of planting is in more inland parts of the country, and this from a greater preparation of the ground and the erection of guards being necessary.

The formation of sea-side plantations has been carried out very successfully in some parts of Scotland, in France, and at the Cape of Good Hope, and although these have, generally speaking, been carried out under very unfavorable circumstances in regard to soil, salt water, and strong winds, several of them have flourished in a remarkable manner, and given every satisfaction. In the Gulf of Garcony, in France, over 13,000 acres of poor open sandy waste have been put under a very thriving crop of *Pinus Pinaster*. This was done by simply sowing the seed of the tree, mixed with seed of the broom (2lbs. of the former to 5lbs. of the latter to an acre) in lines, and covering the ground with pine and furze branches to protect the seed until it germinated, and afterwards until the young plants had attained strength to withstand the vicissitudes of the site. The broom was sown in order to give some shelter to the young pines until they made some headway, when the latter eventually overtopped and killed the former. This system is worth trying here, and I have no doubt but that where the soil is not of too drifty a character, and the site not too much exposed to the direct blasts of the sea, fair results would be obtained by it. It has also been tried with good results on the flats of sand towards Wynberg, at the Cape of Good Hope. There, however, the planting the trees directly into their sites from the nursery has also met with success.

In Scotland, the plantations on sea-side sites are always formed of young plants from the nursery, specially prepared with strong sturdy stems, plenty of fibrous roots, and of a hardy constitution ; and I am of opinion that this is the most certain, and, in the end, expeditious manner of forming plantations of the kind in this country.

I shall now, therefore, give a few general directions as to how the operations connected with the formation of plantations on our sea-coast should be conducted in order to a fairly successful issue.

The Choosing of the Site.—There is, of course, great differences in the soil, subsoil, and exposure of localities on the sea-coast which are not far from one another. This is, I think, more marked as a rule than in inland situations. Some have a good clay-loam throughout, with a fair amount of shelter from the wind by the ground sloping inland from the sea bank; while others have a soil of a very poor drifting sandy loam, with an exposed aspect to the sea. Again, there are the several intermediate sites between these two, so that much variety of material consequence exists in this way. Of course, there may sometimes be a considerable tract of sea-coast which it is desired to have put under a crop of trees, which possesses all the variety of sites named. In any case, however, the site chosen for the first planting operations should be selected with the twofold view of making an encouraging beginning and of affording shelter to other plantations to be afterwards formed.

Preparation of the Soil.—Much of the success will depend upon whether this be done properly or not. Where the soil is of a clayey nature, I would advise that, if practicable, the whole of the ground enclosed be ploughed and subsoiled to a depth of at least sixteen inches. If the soil is naturally of a wet and sour nature, a few open drains should be run through it, so that it may become pervious and sweet to the rootlets of the young trees. The ground having been all dealt with as advised, the next operation will be the opening of the holes for the plants. These should be about two and a-half feet wide on top, two feet in depth, and they ought to be kept open for a month or two before planting, in order that the soil may become thoroughly loose and nicely pulverised before being put round the roots of the trees. In opening the holes, the top soil should be carefully kept on one side, and not mixed with that of the subsoil, and afterwards it should be put as the top covering to the roots, when the trees are planted. Where there is a dense mass of native vegetation, it will be found that considerable difficulty will be experienced in rearing flourishing plantations on the site, as this will take up all the nourishment to the exclusion of the young trees. Where the soil is of a clay nature, this herbage will of course be destroyed by the ploughing, as advised; but where the site is of a sandy nature and liable to drift, the herbage is of course of value to prevent the soil from shifting, and it should therefore be retained. In this case, therefore, it is advisable to destroy the herbage immediately round the plants only, and to leave the ground betwixt the rows in a perfectly undisturbed state. In sandy sites, the holes for the plants need not be opened until planting season; they should, however, be of about the same size as recommended for clayey soils.

Kinds of Trees to Plant.—There is, unfortunately, not a very extensive selection of trees which are known to do well in situations near the sea-coast. Such as I shall give, however, have been well tried in different parts of the world, and may, therefore, be accepted as suitable for the purpose. (See Chapter XXXV. for this list.)

Description of Plants.—For sea-side planting it is necessary to success that the plants used be specially prepared for the purpose, so that they may possess plenty of strong fibrous roots, be well-branched, sturdy, and have a hardy constitution. It would be mere waste of money and labor to plant trees on such sites which have been tenderly reared and nourished. This is a matter of very great importance, and ought never to be neglected in the formation of sea-side plantations. All the *deciduous* trees, and others which will bear moving readily, should be transplanted *twice* in the nursery before they are put out into their permanent sites, and the second operation of this kind ought to be in an open piece of ground, where they should stand well clear of one another in the rows in order that they may get well-branched and symmetrical in shape. Again, where the plants have to be grown in pots, they should be re-potted two or three times, and on each occasion into a pot of a larger size than the previous one. The plants must not be allowed to get pot-bound. Plants of this class should also be reared in the open-air as much as possible, and in an open and somewhat airy place.

When to Plant.—The trees to be planted on such sites, being *Coniferæ* and *Deciduous* kinds chiefly, and hardy, may be put out in their sites immediately after the rains of winter have fairly begun, say about the middle of June; but this, of course, will depend very much upon the local climate of the district in which the planting is to be done. If planted early in the season the trees will have all the better chance of getting settled down into their sites, so that they may be in a position to make an early start in spring, and thus get thoroughly established in the soil before the summer droughts set in.

How to Plant.—Too much care cannot be displayed in the operation of planting the young trees out into their sites. Some nicely prepared soil, with a little manure in it, should be put all round the roots of the plants as they are inserted; indeed, if possible, the holes made for the trees in very sandy sites should be filled up chiefly with prepared soil of

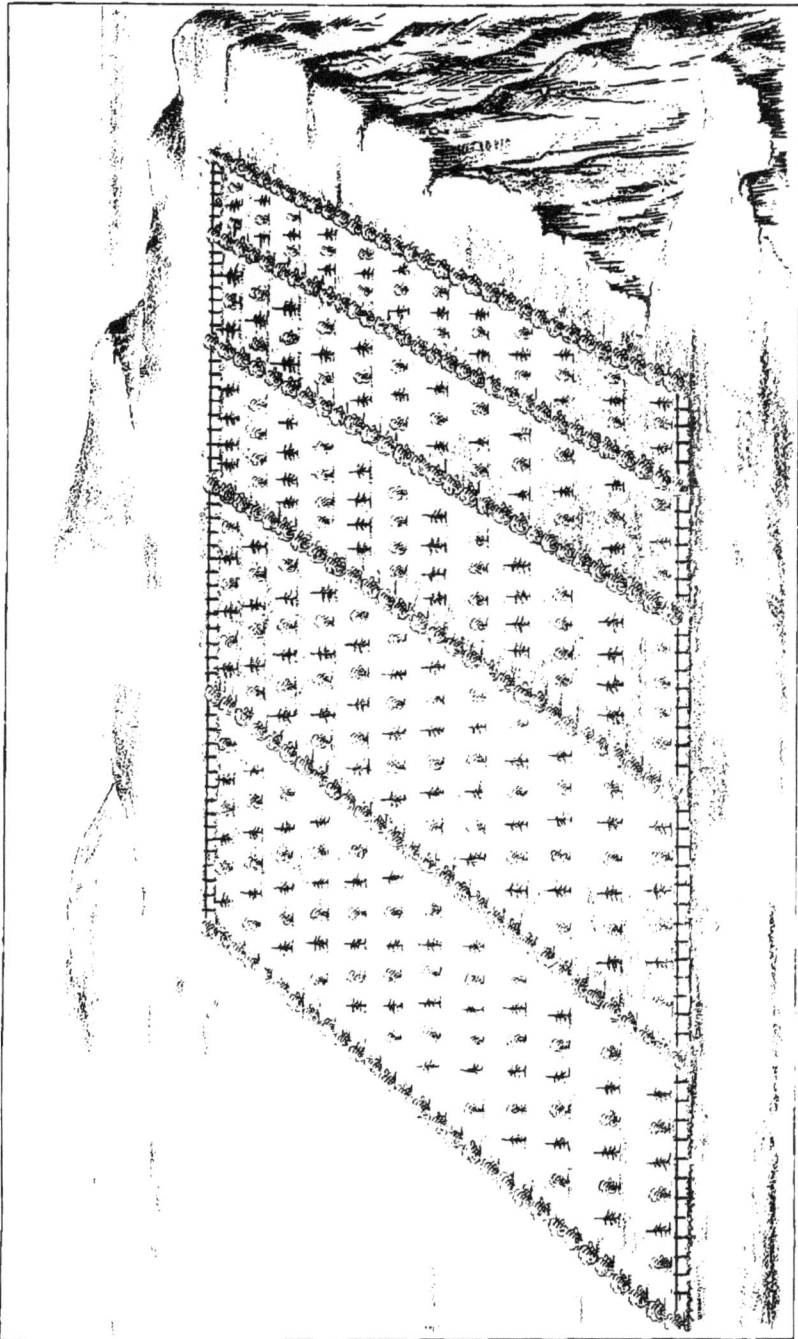

Fig 10.

this kind, together with ordinary black loam. The roots of the trees must *not* be long exposed to the sea breeze, as the small *spongioles* or spongy tissue at the end of the roots, through which nourishment is conveyed to the plant, will otherwise soon get dried up, and failure will follow. The system of " puddling," which is elsewhere explained in these pages, should especially be applied in the treatment of trees for sea-side plantations.

Distance Apart to Plant.—This should not be more than 8ft., plant from plant, in the plantation grounds. On the outside of the plantation, or that nearest the sea, a belt of say one chain in breadth should be formed of commoner kinds of trees and shrubs, put in at 5ft. apart, in order to come up quickly and form a break-wind to the more valuable kinds to leeward.

Break-Winds.—In seaside planting, of whatever description, it is indispensably necessary to protect the young plants for a while until they get established in the ground, and become of such heights and strength as will admit of their resisting the effects of the vicissitudes of the site. There are many ways of doing this ; and of course much will depend on the size of the plantation, as well as the kind of material at hand for the purpose, as to what kind of structure should be erected. One of the best and least expensive materials for the purpose is the common brush-wood which is always to be found on our coasts. This can be worked up into excellent screen-fences by driving stakes into the ground at every 10ft. (these to stand 7ft. out of the ground), with three wires run through them at about 2ft. apart. The brush can then be laced into the wires like hurdle-work, with the ends of the lower tier sunk 6in. or 8in. into the ground. Or it can be piled up to a height of 6ft. to 7ft., in regular bush-fence fashion, with stakes driven into the ground on both sides to keep it stationary. Much, of course, will depend upon the character of the site—whether it be more than usually exposed, or the reverse—as to the number of screen fences which it may be necessary to erect in a plantation, but I can only say that if the brushwood is plentiful, the more fences there are put up the better will it undoubtedly be for the young trees. The first and largest fence should be run close to the sea-margin of the plantation, and in a line parallel with the sea-line ; the second fence parallel to the first, and about 200ft. from it ; the third, 300ft. from the second ; the fourth, 500ft. from the third (each time increasing the distance between the fences as they get further from the coast) ; and so on through the whole plantation if it is very much exposed, or, if it is not of this character, until fairly sheltered ground is reached, when the screen may be discontinued altogether. In very sandy sites, where there is likely to be a drift, bushes should be laid all over the surface of the ground until the plants get a fair size and cover the space betwixt the rows.

In Fig. 10 I give a rough sketch of plantation on sea-coast, showing brush-screens as described above.

Cleaning and Mulching.—The soil should be frequently stirred about the roots of the young trees, and afterwards carefully mulched before summer, all in the manner elsewhere described in this work.

CHAPTER XVIII.

Osier Planting.

THERE are many spots in the colony where osiers could be grown to great advantage and profit to the owner. At present the making of basket-ware is not one of our industries, but when we think of the large number of baskets which could be utilised in the shipping of fruit and potatoes to our local and foreign markets, it is, I think, a matter of surprise that the subject has not been taken up before now. Feeling convinced, however, that it will ere long receive that amount of public attention which it here deserves, I devote a short chapter to some recommendations regarding the formation of *osier beds*.

The *Osiers* (salix—from the Celtic *sal*, near, and *lix*, water) are a genus of plants indigenous chiefly to the continents of Europe and America. The family is a very numerous one, and possesses many varieties closely allied to one another. The term "willow" is applied to the same genus. Some members of the family attain to the size of trees, and produce timber valuable for works requiring soft woods.

The species most suitable for the purpose of osier plantations in this country are the following :—

Salix Viminalis, or common osier.—This is the common willow of Europe, and is extensively cultivated as an osier. For wickerwork and hoop-making the shoots are unequalled. A rapid grower, and easily propagated from cuttings.

Salix Stipularis, or the auricle-leaved osier.—In Holland this species is largely cultivated for the making of hoops and rods.

Salix Rubra, or green-leaved osier.—A very tough species, now in general use, and a rapid grower ; suitable for crates, basket, and wickerwork.

Salix Forbyana, the fine basket osier. A strong, pliable, and easily worked species ; valuable for the finer sorts of wickerwork.

Salix Triandra, the long-leaved osier.—This is a very common kind, and is grown for basket and hoop-making. Shoots grow 9ft. long in one season.

Salix Purpurea, or the bitter willow.—A very tough willow, and used for withes and baskets. It is bitter to the taste, and hence is not liable to be eaten by insects. This kind will grow in sites constantly covered with water. Prefers soils somewhat light, and not retentive or clayey. In suitable spots makes a quick-growing and valuable hedge or screen.

Osiers must have plenty of moisture to succeed well and grow to perfection. Unless they have this, it is useless to attempt to grow them. They succeed best upon soils of a deep, loose, strong loam, with a retentive subsoil, such as we invariably find where water lodges. They also, however, grow well on soils of a poorer and lighter character, so long as there is plenty of moisture in the subsoil, although, in this case, the crop will not be in such bulk and to such perfection as in the other case referred to. An excellent site for an osier bed is on a flat with high grounds all round it, from which moisture is supplied to the plants by gravitation. Perhaps, however, the best site of all is on the banks of a river near the sea, which are subject to tidal overflow. On such a site the beds are supplied with plenty of water and manure in the shape of mud-sediment, from which cause a great growth ensues, and notwithstanding frequent cuttings, no deterioration of the crop takes place.

As a rule, osier beds, if properly planted and managed, will last from 30 to 70 years, according to the quality of the soil, without renovation, except by occasional mending. In this remark I, of course, refer to my experience of osier plantations in Europe; but at the same time, I think that the remark will apply to them in this country as well.

The preparation of the ground previous to its being planted is an important matter to the after success of the crop. No expense should, therefore, be spared in order to give it full justice in this respect. The soil must be made loose, and entirely free from obstructions in the way of stones, tree-roots, &c., &c.; and in order to do this, it should be carefully trenched to a depth of from 18 to 24in. In very wet and cold places the ground should be drained.

The ground properly prepared, as advised above, the osiers may then be inserted in their sites. It is usual to put cuttings in instead of plants, and these should consist of strong young wood, about ½in. to 1in. thick, and about 15in. to 18in. in length. The cuttings should be procured at the season of the year when the trees have cast their leaves and their vitality is in a dormant state.

The sets should be inserted in the ground to a depth of from 10in. to 12in., and placed in rows 2ft. to 2½ft. apart, with the sets 18in. from one another in the rows. It is absolutely necessary to plant them at this short distance apart, in order that the shoots may become straight and slender, and therefore fit for the purposes of basket-making.

If the shoots are not very strong the first year, they should be allowed to remain for a season in order to strengthen the stocks. In cutting the first crop, care must be taken to leave several buds on the stocks. In after-cuttings the shoots should be removed close to those parts. Of course, as to how long they should remain on the stock, much will depend upon the purpose for which the shoots are intended; if for common basket-work, one year's growth will suffice; but if they are to be used for hoop-making, &c., two, and perhaps three years' growth will be necessary.

The crop should be cut after the leaves have fallen.

After the crop has been removed, the ground all round the stocks should be dug, manured, and otherwise carefully attended to.

CHAPTER XIX.

Planting on Ground lately Cleared of Trees.

TREES must be looked upon by the forester in many respects the same as the farmer views a cereal crop. No intelligent agriculturist would think for a moment of cropping a piece of ground with the same kind of plant for several years without some period of rest to the land, in order to return somewhat of the various constituents taken from it by his crop. We, of course, know it is done, but then we are also painfully aware what the result is. Land cropped with trees or wheat—it matters not which it may be—requires some systematic course of treatment after one crop is taken from it before another is made to take its place.

Where trees have stood thickly for a long series of years upon a piece of ground, and then felled, it is found that from the large deposit of vegetable substances upon the soil, together with the fact that it has not had the salubrious influences of the sunlight upon it for many years, the site has become somewhat uncongenial to the health and growth of a younger crop of trees. In this country, the crop of indigenous trees is, generally speaking, very sparse upon the ground, and consequently, plenty of light penetrates through the foliage to the soil; there is less fear therefore of bad results flowing from replanting ground here which has been recently denuded of its crop of trees. It may have been noticed, however, that where *eucalypti* have grown for any great length of time, the soil becomes hard and of a sour and uninviting appearance round the trees; it is therefore generally unsuitable for early replanting. The roots of old trees and stumps are a means of encouraging insects on the ground, which attack the young trees and prey so much upon their vitality that they become of a very sickly appearance, and eventually die.

After the ground has been cleared of its old crop, the branches and other *debris* left should be spread over the part, so as not to have too much of it upon any one spot, and at a suitable season the whole should be thoroughly burned. Where by chance any fire of more than ordinary size has occurred, the ash deposited upon the site should be spread over the adjoining ground, so that no heavy deposit of it is left upon any one spot. This is necessary, as, although a small quantity of ash is of great service to young plants, a heavy dose of it will kill them.

This done, I would advise that the ground be then thoroughly ploughed as far as possible to a good depth, and afterwards summer-fallowed (say by two ploughings and harrowings) one or two seasons, in accordance with whether the old crop was thick upon the ground or not. If the ground cannot well be spared lying idle for such a length of time, it may be cropped once with nice clean wheat, which should be taken off in the form of hay, and then ploughed, harrowed, and ploughed again that season before it is planted with trees. By this time the soil will have become nicely mellowed, and the rain having percolated through it charged with the sweetening and renovating gases from the atmosphere, it will now be fit for planting purposes once more.

Where the situation is of such a character as will not admit of its being ploughed and treated in the manner just described, the following mode of procedure must be adopted :—

After the site has been freed of all the branches and other rubbish left upon it from the old crop, holes or pits for the young trees should be prepared as early as possible, so that they may lay open for a period of not less than three or four months before planting. In making these pits great care should be exercised to see that all the old roots are removed for some distance round the space to be occupied by each plant, and that they are at once burned or otherwise removed from the ground. These pits ought not to be less than 30in. square on top, and about 20in. in depth. Should the ground be more than usually hard round the spaces thus opened for the plants. it should be loosened on the surface with the pick for a breadth of about 2ft. round each hole. The plants used in a plantation of this kind, where the soil cannot be ploughed, should be of the very best description and possess plenty of fibrous roots, with a fine strong and healthy habit throughout.

CHAPTER XX.

———⟨∘⟩———

Town and Park Planting.

THERE is perhaps nothing which gives so much pleasure to people residing in towns and cities as trees planted along the streets and other thoroughfares. The shade received from them makes the walks cool, and the bright glare which is so trying to the eyes is mellowed down to such a degree that walking in the busy streets in the noon-day heat becomes bearable, and even pleasant, to all. Moreover, the effect of having the thoroughfares of our cities lined with arboreous growths would be to purify and regulate the condition of the air, and thus make it suitable for the healthy residence of the people. Trees are very searching and wonderful scavengers, and their leaves so act upon and assimilate deleterious gases arising from the gregarious habits of men, that many epidemic diseases consequent upon atmospheric disturbances are frequently prevented by them.

That happy and beneficial results would flow to the city and towns of South Australia, if trees were planted regularly and systematically along both sides of the streets and roads, there can be no question of doubt. Indeed, with the climate which we possess, the general good which would arise from this would be far greater than we are at present really alive to. It is most gratifying, therefore, to find that the spirit of the age in regard to tree-planting is upon us, and that the municipal bodies of several of our largest centres of population are making praiseworthy efforts to make them "a thing of beauty and a joy for ever." Prominent among these I have pleasure in naming, besides our fine city of Adelaide, the townships of Jamestown, Gladstone, Port Pirie, Port Augusta, Strathalbyn, Gawler, and Kapunda.

The rearing of trees of a character suitable for planting in streets and avenues generally, the manner in which they should be dealt with when planted into their sites, and their management afterwards, requiring very special treatment, I shall devote this chapter to giving some hints on the various matters connected with the subject as a whole, for the guidance of our municipal bodies and others.

Under another heading of this work will be found a list of the kinds of trees which I consider suitable for street-planting generally. I am strongly of the opinion—which is derived from Parisian, and American experience in New York, Philadelphia, Montreal, and Toronto, of such matters—that *deciduous* trees are, as a rule, better suited for planting in our streets than those of an evergreen habit. In the cities named, such

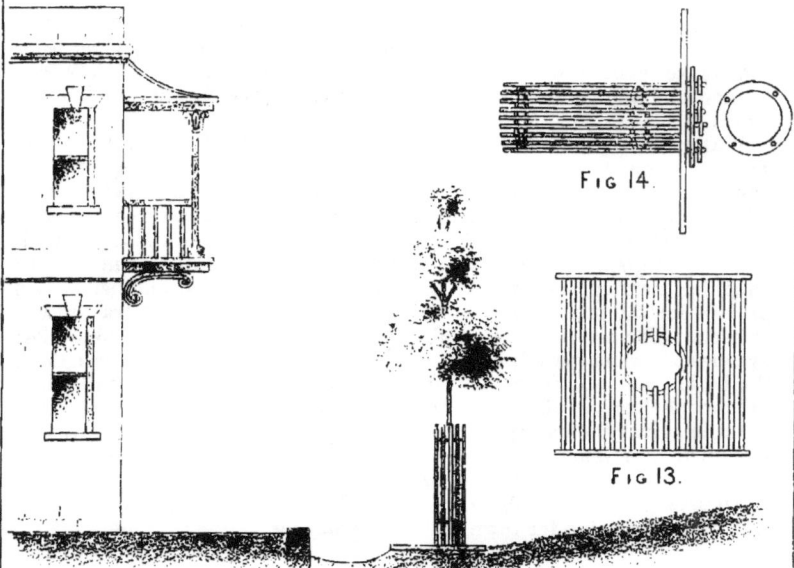

Fig 14.

Fig 13.

Fig 11.

Fig 12.

Figs 11, 12, and 14. Trees planted in this manner require constant pruning in order to keep them within proper bounds, and at the same time make them of a nice regular shape. No pruning should, however, be done by anyone unless he is a man thoroughly up to this kind of work.

Incalculable good could be done to the general condition of the townships throughout the country were planting carried out extensively and systematically on their park lands. Every means should, therefore, be adopted by their inhabitants to have this done. Trees for ornamental planting of this kind should be strong and hardy, well-balanced, well-rooted, and good in every other respect. They should be planted in an irregular manner, and at such distances apart one from another as will provide for the proper expansion and development of the characteristics of each. The plantations should consist of belts with sinuous boundaries; avenues along footpaths; and clumps artistically interspersed throughout the parks; and all so arranged that the most will be made of the site to produce shelter and pleasure to the inhabitants. In Fig. 15 I give a sketch of an imaginary township and park lands planted in the way referred to, from which, perhaps, some of our corporate bodies may get an idea in regard to the planting of the lands under their control.

Figures 16, 17, 18, 19, 20, 21, 22, and 23, represent a few forms of tree guards suitable for town and park planting.

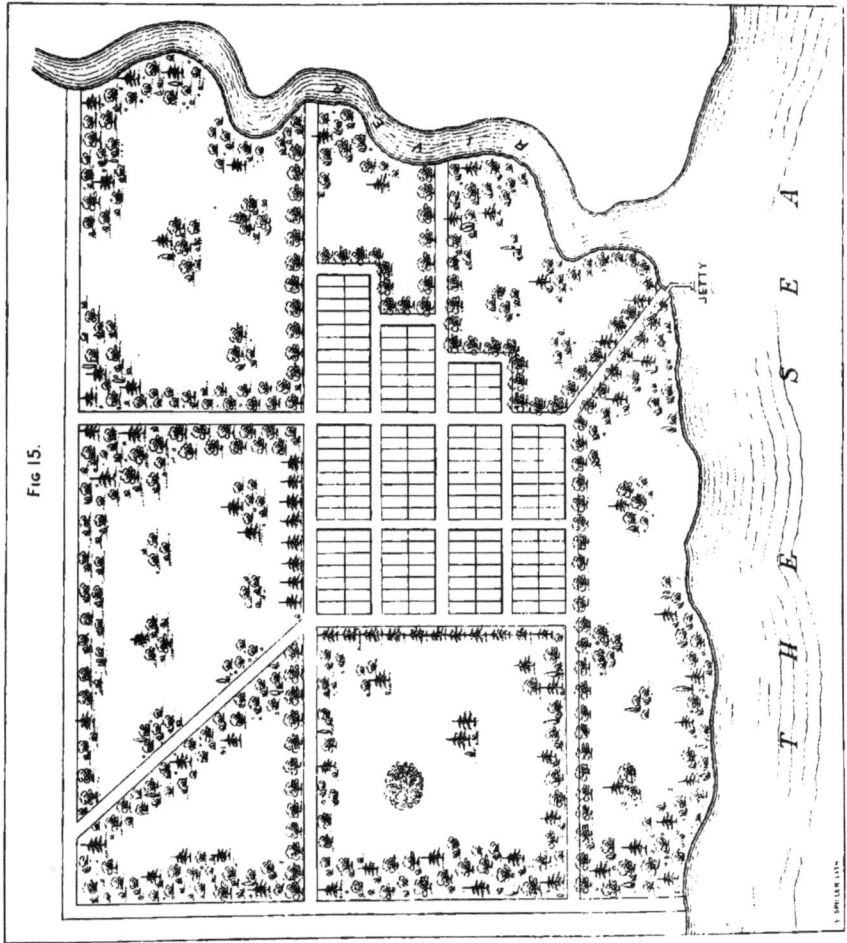

Fig 15.

Fig 16

Fig 17.

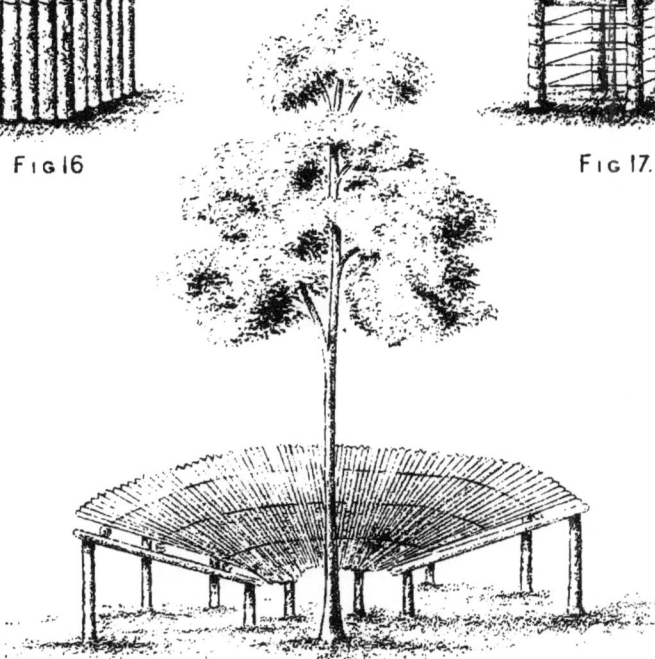

Fig 18.

Fig 19

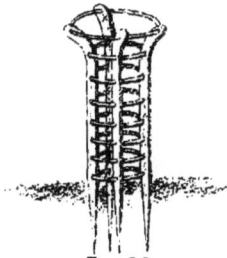

Fig 20

Fig 21.

Fig 22

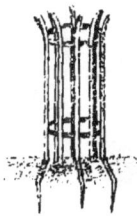

Fig 23.

E. SPILLER LITH.

CHAPTER XXI.

Wattle Growing.

THE several industries which are intimately connected with the bark question here—such as those of the growers of the raw material, the strippers, tanners, fellmongers, leather exporters, and others, with their various collateral dependencies, form such an array of important and minor branches of political economy, that it is obvious the subject of a regular and permanent supply of bark is a matter which deserves the best attention of our legislators. Not only should it be seen that the supply at present required shall be kept up without any falling off, but also that the best endeavours be made in order that the several industries named are developed and increased in the colony.

The stripping of wattle-bark has been a common source of livelihood to many ever since the foundation of the colony, but of late years this industry has sensibly decreased, from the fact that the country is being gradually taken up for settlement, whereby the forests of wattles are being slowly but surely diminished in extent, and those left are stripped of young trees to such an extent that the proper reproduction of the crop is hindered. The annual output of bark is consequently diminished. As the country gets further settled and put under cultivation or stock, the supply is sure to suffer still more, and if nothing be done towards cultivating the wattle, it may eventually decline to such an extent as effectually to damage the industries in our midst connected with the bark, as well as, of course, diminish its export from the colony.

Very few large fields of wattles are now to be seen in the colony, except on the Waste Lands of the Crown and on a few of the largest of our landed properties. The Forest Board is now taking active steps towards the conservation of existing wattles, and the rearing of these in special plantations where the soil and situation are not entirely suitable for the growth of timber trees.

We are of course aware that wattles spring up spontaneously in different parts of the colony; and while admitting the value of this to the country, and at the same time recognising the fact that by this means a crop of this tree can generally be got simply by protection from stock, we must also admit the fact that crops of this kind are somewhat uncertain, and that there are places where the wattle does not grow naturally which might be put under a profitable plantation of the tree by artificial means. It is not too much to say, that on almost every farm in the country there are one or more spots on which wattles might be

E

grown with great advantage and profit to their owners without interfering with the really available cropping land of the farm. Besides,
such spots could then be made to present a fine clothed appearance,
which are at present of an unsightly character in the landscape. While,
therefore, pointing out to our farmers the advantages of planting timber-
trees on their farms, I cannot miss this opportunity to strongly advocate
the formation by them of wattle plantations as well. These are easy and
cheap of formation, they fill up poor and unsightly spots as I have
already pointed out, and what is also of considerable importance, the
returns from them are quick and valuable.

I consider this matter of such importance that I will now endeavor to
give some general instructions in regard to the formation of wattle
plantations.

In a few years' time, after proper trial, I hope to see many kinds of
trees cultivated in the colony for the purpose of yielding tannin-
producing bark, but I question if anything we can introduce will be
able to compete with the bark of our indigenous wattles. This is
so rich in tannic acid that it readily sells in the European market at
from £12 to £16 per ton. It is said to be 50 per cent. more valuable
in tannin than the bark of oak or larch; and I am aware that it
realises fully one-half more per ton than anything grown at home.
Moreover, if we also look at the more rapid rate of growth of the
wattle than of the exotic trees, there is much to be said in favor of
the cultivation of the former.

Those wattles which I more particularly refer to, and which yield
the mimosa bark of commerce, are:—

Acacia pycnantha, or the common broad-leaved wattle of the colony.
It grows from 15ft. to 25ft. in height, and from 8in. to 10in. in diameter
at the base. The period of maturity may be put down at from seven to
ten years, but the bark contains most tannin when the tree is about five
to six years old. The tree grows on all kinds of soils. This is the most
valuable of our wattles, and the bark produces from 30 to 35 per cent.
of tannin.

Acacia decurrens, or the common black wattle.—This is a tree of
much quicker growth, and one which attains to larger dimensions of
timber than *A. pycnantha*. In five or six years' time it will attain a
height of 40ft. and from 12in. to 24in. in diameter. It can be stripped
when four or five years old, or sooner, if necessary. Grows upon all
sorts of soils, but seems to do best on those of a sandy-loam character.
The bark produces from 20 to 33 per cent. of tannic acid.

Wattles may very judiciously be grown (1st) on poor spots where
timber trees will not grow to profitable dimensions; (2nd) in masses, on
exposed parts, so as to act as shelter to more valuable trees to leeward;
and (3rd) as " nurses" on certain spots, so as to protect and encourage
the growth of timber trees which are intended to occupy the ground
as the permanent crop.

In order to expedite and cheapen, as much as possible, the operation
of forming wattle plantations, it is necessary that the seeds of the trees
be sown on the sites which the plants are to occupy. Both of the species

named grow so freely from the seed that no difficulty will be experienced in getting a crop of them established on the ground by this process. This will, however, require to be done in such a manner that the different operations of pruning, thinning. and clearing can be executed in a systematic manner. My views on the subject, in order to this, are as follows :—

Preparation of the Seed.—Wattle seed being hard and not easily germinated, it should be made soft before being sown. This can be best done by placing it in *almost* boiling water and then leaving it to soak for forty-eight hours, and afterwards sweating it in a damp bag until quite soft.

Sowing Wattle in masses by themselves.—In order to ensure regularity of growth as much as possible, and, consequently, fitness of the whole crop for thinning and clearing at regular periods, I would advise that each species be sown in blocks by itself.

On those portions which are intended to be put under masses of any of the *acacias* named, and which are not of too hilly and rough a character to allow of the ground being properly worked, the plough should be used in opening it up for the reception of the seed.

In order that the trees may come up in a regular manner, furrows should be opened parallel to one another all over the ground to be sown, at 3ft. to 4ft. apart, in as straight lines as the character of the ground will admit of.

This all done, men, provided with seed in bags, will go along the opened furrows and drop a few seeds in at every 2ft. or 3ft.; the second man dropping the seed in his row one pace behind the first man, the third man doing the same in his row one pace behind the second man, and so on throughout the whole ground to be operated on.

By this simple plan, the trees will be alternate in the rows, and be from 2ft. to 3ft. apart over all; and by their branches meeting regularly on all sides of them, they will be confined, and their vitality consequently concentrated more to making stem than side shoots.

When the ground comes to be operated on for stripping purposes, which would be after the fifth year, and by thinnings extending over two or three years, as the nature of the tree and its general conditions would admit of, a certain number of good healthy trees should be left on the ground in order to supply seed for another crop; and thus, once fairly established, the operations of seeding and clearing would go on regularly year after year without intermission.

Sowing Wattles as "Nurses" to Timber Trees.—On those portions of a plantation where the wattles would come in as nurses to more valuable timber trees, the operations of planting and sowing should be conducted as follows :—

Let the plough first open straight furrows all over the ground at 4ft. apart, and parallel to one another, as in the case already referred to. This all done, the next process will be the planting of the more valuable kinds of trees which are to remain in the ground as the permanent crop. These should consist of such kinds as the character of the soil and the nature of the site will indicate as are likely to succeed best upon it. The selection made, men will go along each furrow and prepare spaces for the plants, say at 8ft. apart. The young trees having been planted in these places, the filling up of the ground with the wattles, or nurses, should now be gone about. This should be done by the men going along each furrow and dropping in seed at about 2ft. apart. These operations all completed, the ground will now be planted with young trees 8ft. apart, and sown with wattles as nurses to 2ft., plant from plant, over all the ground.

Putting in a Wattle Crop with the Spade.—There will, of course, be certain spots on a farm which it may be advisable to put under a crop of wattles, but which are of too rough a character generally to admit of the plough being used on them in order to stir up the soil sufficiently for the proper covering of the seed. In such cases the spade will have to be employed for this purpose.

In preparing the ground for the reception of the seed by this system, the men will, first of all, go along and stir up the soil to about a spade's breadth, at from 2 to 3ft. apart, over all the ground, and those of one row to alternate with those of the other next to it, as in the manner already described. This all done satisfactorily, the seed can be sown as already described.

Management of Wattle Plantations.—We will suppose that plantations of wattle have been formed as described, and that a fair crop of young plants is the result. The first operation of management which will have to be attended to is that of going along each row and thinning out the weakly and most unpromising plants from each space sown, so as to leave one good strong plant only in each to form the crop upon the ground.

As soon as the young plants left from the thinning operation, described above, have begun to grow freely, it will be necessary to go over them once more and do what pruning is required, in order to direct their growth into one stem as much as possible. This will be the means of producing more bark, and make it easier of being stripped at maturity.

Beyond paying attention to keeping the roads ploughed in the summer time, so as to avoid risk from fire, no further expense need be incurred in these plantations, until the period arrives for the first general thinning operation upon them.

No definite period can be stated here as to when the trees will be in the condition necessary for the first thinning. This will depend altogether upon the species of wattle grown, and the growth of the plants throughout. As a rule, however, where they have been healthy and of vigorous growth, we may calculate upon this coming off about the fifth or sixth year after the period of sowing.

Bark containing the most tannic acid is that stripped from trees between the ages of five and eight years.

The first thinning should consist of every alternate tree in the rows. This would then leave those remaining on the ground at from 4ft. to 6ft. apart over all.

A period of two years will now elapse before the same part can be operated on again for stripping purposes. Thinning again the year immediately following the first operation would be injudicious, and a waste of material.

When the trees are seven years old, therefore, they will have to be again dealt with for stripping purposes. In doing this, it will be matter for observation on the ground as to whether a thinning only should be done at this time, or that a complete clearance of the whole of the remaining trees should take place. No rule can be laid down for this, as it might be found, on an inspection of the plantation, that the trees had come to maturity, and that to leave any of them on the ground for another year would only be the means of deteriorating the commercial value of the bark, and therefore occupying the ground unprofitably; while again, it might be that a thinning simply would be not only an advantage to the district at large, in order to leave some trees on the ground for shelter, but it might be better in a pecuniary sense as well were the trees still in rapid growth and therefore daily putting on a greater bulk of good bark.

Again, from the different habitats of the wattles named, we shall probably find that one will have arrived at maturity long before the other has attained the period of its most vigorous growth. In this case it would be absurd to lay down a rule as applicable to both. This, therefore, is a matter for settlement on the ground.

Once get a crop of wattles fairly established on the ground, and it is my opinion that no difficulty will afterwards be encountered in keeping up a regular crop of them on the ground by natural reproduction.

CHAPTER XXII.

Pruning Forest Trees.

THE pruning of forest trees is a work which, if judiciously and carefully executed, will repay in after years fifty-fold the expense put upon it. Of its utility there can be no doubt; but it is a branch of forestry which requires years of training and observation to execute with judgment and advantage to the crop being operated on. Men not accustomed to the work are apt, without thought, and from their not knowing better, to materially damage a plantation of trees by what may simply be called *injudicious pruning.*

In the arboricultural world with which we come in contact, there are found men who advocate severe pruning; others, that the operation should be carried on upon a moderate scale; and others again who say that pruning should not be done at all. For my own part I must say that experience has advised me to recommend the *moderate pruning* of trees only.

There can be no greater mistake made in the rearing of plantations than that of severe and indiscriminate pruning. There is, I think, a mania for this sort of thing with many people in this country. How often do we find fine, healthy, and well-balanced trees for ever spoiled by the too-free use of the knife? I can point to a case where I was invited in to see what was described as a "magnificent" specimen of a year-old Tasmanian Bluegum tree. On inspection, I found a *whipstick*-looking affair, about 12ft. high, all the branches pruned off close to the trunk, and the stem itself not more than *one inch* in diameter. This was a case of *very injudicious* pruning to a certainty. It must not be forgotten that the leaves act as stomachs to plants, and that therefore, if too large an amount of leaf surface is removed from a tree, this is sure to have a very injurious effect upon its health.

Of course, because mistakes of this kind are made, there is no reason why these should weigh against the judicious application of the system. They only serve as beacons, warning us against their repetition.

It has now been clearly proved, after a long period of years of experiments, that judicious pruning improves the quality of the timber at maturity, as against that which has been allowed to grow in accordance with nature. This was ascertained by selecting two blocks of plantation close to one another, planted at the same time, and with the same kinds of trees. One portion was carefully pruned and thinned and otherwise properly seen to, while the other portion was allowed to take its own course. At maturity, the trees of both were cut, with the result that the portion which had been regularly looked after produced a much more valuable sample and a larger quantity of timber than the other.

Pruning, in my opinion, is simply a means to assist nature to produce fine straight wood, and a larger quantity of it. With lots of large gnarled branches upon a tree, the timber is always of an inferior quality. This holds good with reference to all trees, more or less, as the case may be, and I think especially so with regard to the *Eucalypti*. Look at the trees in the greater portion of the natural forests of this colony! Don't we find them, as a rule, composed chiefly of great heavy branches and a small thick-set trunk? And when they are cut down, is not more than two-thirds of the whole bulk of the tree made up of branches and limbs which have grown upon the tree to the detriment of the stem? Now, had it been possible to have looked after the trees when in their young state, there would now have been more than 80 per cent. of good marketable timber in each tree in our forests, instead of only about 30 per cent. as they now stand.

Of course, where trees are planted thickly, there is little or no necessity for pruning. Nature then becomes her own pruner; and by the attention of the forester to timely thinning, the energies of the trees are constantly directed to the stem, and an upward growth is maintained; thus producing a straight stem and well-grown timber. When trees are grown closely together, the leading shoot of each tree naturally seeks the light, and this having acquired an ascendancy over the others, becomes in time the trunk of the tree; and from the shading and pressure of the other trees all round, the inferior shoots cannot make headway and so they gradually decline in health and die off. And so the same course follows on year after year as the trees push upwards, until at last, in the course of years, we find magnificent trees, with stems 80ft. to 100ft. without a branch, and producing timber *free* of knots, and of the very best description of timber throughout.

Under these circumstances, and with this fact before us, can it be wondered at that on every possible occasion I urge upon those about to plant to *do so thickly*. This will save the expense of keeping men pruning each year, and the timber grown will far surpass that produced from trees pruned with the knife—which operation will be necessary if thin planting is adopted with the ultimate view of the trees being felled for timber.

In the young crop of our indigenous forests of the present day, much and really permanent good can be done to the trees by pruning. I would therefore advise those having any forest land left, to attend to the young trees in it. In a few years the result will more than repay any expense incurred in doing so. In these indigenous forests of ours, it will be found that the young crop comes up in a very patchy and straggling manner, and that, therefore, a little careful and judicious pruning is necessary in order to keep the trees from becoming branchy and to a large extent worthless. Work of this kind has been and is now being done by the Forest Board on their reserves, with most beneficial and satisfactory results to the future value of the timber in the forests.

To put the matter as concisely as possible, I would mention the following as a few of the benefits to be derived from a judicious system of pruning in forest lands generally:—Larger and more valuable dimensions of timber in each individual tree ; a larger and surer crop upon an equal area of land; freer circulation amongst the trees, and consequently cleaner stems and less liability to diseases arising from insects, &c.; much quicker returns, because the trees will grow larger and quicker when thus confined and shaded ; the timber is less liable to be shaken in the grain than when the trees are growing openly and thus exposed to the influence of the winds at all times ; and the timber is freer of knots and other imperfections.

As a rule, I decidedly object to the pruning of *Coniferous* trees, such as pines, cypresses, and junipers. This is, I find, frequently done in the colony, and very much to the injury of the trees, both in a commercial and picturesque point of view. To my mind, there is nothing which creates a greater eyesore, and displays a larger amount of ignorance in the physiology of a pine, than to see it denuded of its branches, and the mutilated and bleeding stem showing signs of decay and unhealthiness; yet this is daily to be seen in our metropolis and in places where certainly better things would be expected.

It is, of course, sometimes necessary to cut out a limb of a pine where two leaders are forming, or to remove dead branches and broken limbs; but beyond some attention in this way, the pruning of trees of this class should be left to nature by close planting only, as she has a way of her own of "choking" off the lower branches of *Coniferæ* without detriment to the future prospects of the tree as a timber producer, which the knife in the hands of man can never do in so efficient a manner.

It may safely be accepted as a point of management in forestry, that nearly all of our *deciduous* trees will bear the application of the knife. At the same time it must be borne in mind, that close planting is, with this class of tree also, the safest and most efficacious manner by which to curtail the branches. From nature's hands in this way we secure the best and straightest timber. While this is the case, however, I would endeavor to impress upon my readers the difference, in a pruning point of view, between *deciduous* and *coniferous* kinds of trees, in so far as the operation affects the health of the trees and the quality of their timber. With the former, then, in these respects the knife can be used with all freedom, but with the latter the reverse is the case.

With some kinds of deciduous trees, the plantations would often become complete failures if pruning were not instituted upon them. We often find this the case with such trees as elms, sycamores, and oaks.

These often take a stunted habit after being a few years in the ground and make no appearance of pushing themselves forward. In such circumstances it is found to be advantageous to the crop to cut all the trees down to the ground. After this is done, a strong growth appears which far exceeds the usual growth of such kinds of trees in ordinary health. I have already had striking examples of this with the redgum of the colony, where stunted and diseased-looking trees have

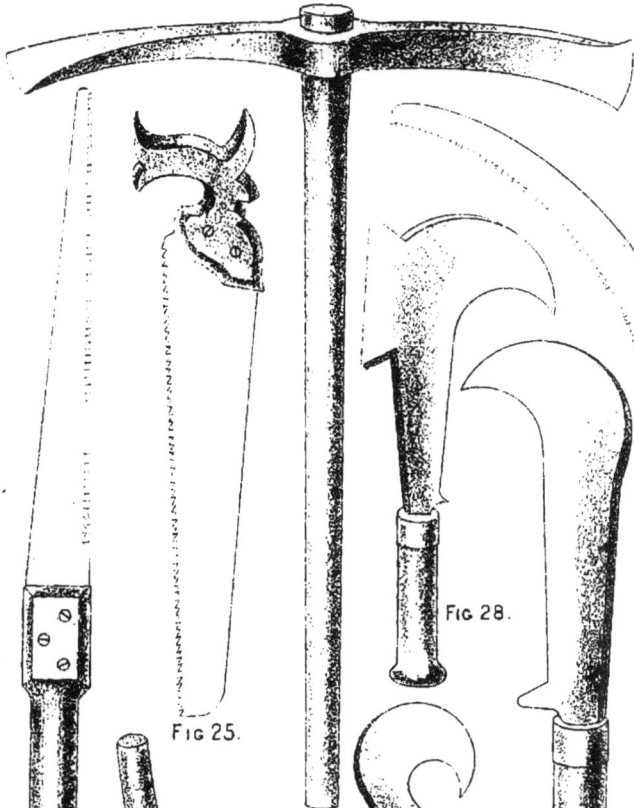

Fig 28.

Fig 25.

Fig 27.

Fig 30

Fig 26

Fig 29.

Fig 31.

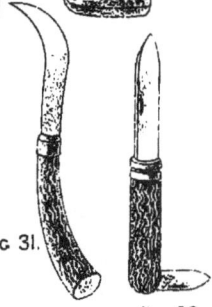

Fig 33.

Fig 24

Fig 32.

E. SPILLER, LITH.

been cut down, and fresh growths have grown up from the stumps far exceeding in one year what the old stunted tree had taken several years to attain.

If pruning be done at all in a plantation it ought, by all means, to be performed when the trees are young and before their branches have formed any heart-wood. This is a most important point in judicious forest management which it would be well for all planters to be made well aware of. When pruning is done at this stage of the tree's growth, the wound quickly heals up and no damage is done to the quality of the timber. Besides, when branches are cut from a tree when young, these can be taken off close to the bark of the stem without any risk of injury to the tree. In pruning branches of this size the common pruning knife (Fig. 30) should be used, and the cut made upwards so that a nice smooth surface may be left free of any roughness upon which water could lodge. Fig. 34 shows where a branch has been taken off cleanly, and Fig. 35 represents the work done in a rough and slovenly manner.

Young deciduous trees should, as much as possible, be pruned before they leave the nursery. This remark has reference, of course, only to such trees as may be in the nursery lines for two or more years; but where one-year-old trees are removed out into the plantations, any large and straggling branches on these should only be shortened back to about 6in. to 10in. from the stem (see Fig. 36), as it is necessary that they be left in order to assist in taking up and elaborating the sap for the formation of woody matter during the following season. If the young trees are severely pruned and planted out the same season, a good deal of bleeding takes place at the wounds, and a lot of objectionable young shoots are formed; besides, there is a chance of the top of the tree dying off from the want of sufficient *stomacha* to keep up the flow of sap. Plantations formed under such circumstances seldom or never give satisfaction.

When it is thought desirable to remove branches of a larger size than those just referred to, these should be shortened only, as represented in Fig. 37. All that is required in cases of this kind, is simply the checking of the larger branches in order that they may not interfere with the proper growth and symmetry of the tree.

It will sometimes be found that trees have become very branchy from long neglect, thereby interfering with the proper expansion and straightness of the trunk. In this case, it is advisable to trim up the best of them only, by checking any strong side branches which are getting too much ahead of the others, and where there are two or more leading shoots, these should be reduced to one only, choosing of course in all cases the strongest and best in every respect as the shoot to carry on the stem of the plant. Where, however, the trees have become so branchy and ill-shaped that they will never make good timber trees, I would advise their being cut down to the ground, and fresh and straight growths encouraged from the stocks.

It may safely be concluded that, as a rule, where much pruning is found to be necessary in a plantation, there has been some mismanagement in the planting operations, and to this, no doubt, the branchy and spreading habits of the trees may be traced. When trees are planted in congenial soil, and only such put out on any particular site as are known to be suited to its general condition, pruning to any great extent will seldom be required. From this small matter alone, therefore, it will be seen how absolutely necessary it is that the planter should be thoroughly up in his work, so that in the formation of plantations the young trees may be inserted in such sites, and under such special conditions as will leave no doubt as to their general vigor and success, without much attention and care.

As a rule, it is unsafe to cut off a branch close to the stem of a size larger than from 3in. to 4in. in diameter ; and even when this is done, the tree should be in good health and have a stem at least ten times the girth of the branch so operated on.

As a rule, it may be considered that the best season of the year for close pruning is from about the middle of summer to the beginning of autumn. However, for such operations as shortening only, this may be done at all seasons of the year with perfect safety.

A tree should never be stripped clean of its branches for the greater part of its height, leaving only a small tuft of branches on the top. This of course can be done with greater liberty where the trees are thick upon the ground and well sheltered, but as a rule every tree ought to be well-proportioned in its branches to the length of its stem. About one-third branches and two-thirds clean stem, is the right proportion where trees have been pruned. Heavy heads are also objectionable, as these often produce inferior timber by wind-shakes.

Every grower of trees should be aware of this—that "the finest-grained timber is that upon which no lateral branches are allowed to attain a large size." This is a fact which, if carefully thought over and studied, will of itself teach one more in regard to what proper pruning admits of than a whole volume written upon the subject.

Figures 24, 25, 26, 27, 28, 29, 30, 31, 32, and 33 show some of the tools required for pruning purposes. These will explain themselves and require no description.

In Fig. 38 I show a tree of our natural forests as the young growth comes up and is left to nature, and in Fig. 39 is represented the same tree arrived at maturity. Again, in Fig. 40 I give the same growth pruned and cared for, and in Fig. 41 what it may be expected to arrive at at the same period after this attention. This is no exaggerated picture, but is perfectly truthful, and goes to show how important the operation of pruning is if properly applied.

Fıg 36.

Fıg 34.

Fıg 35.

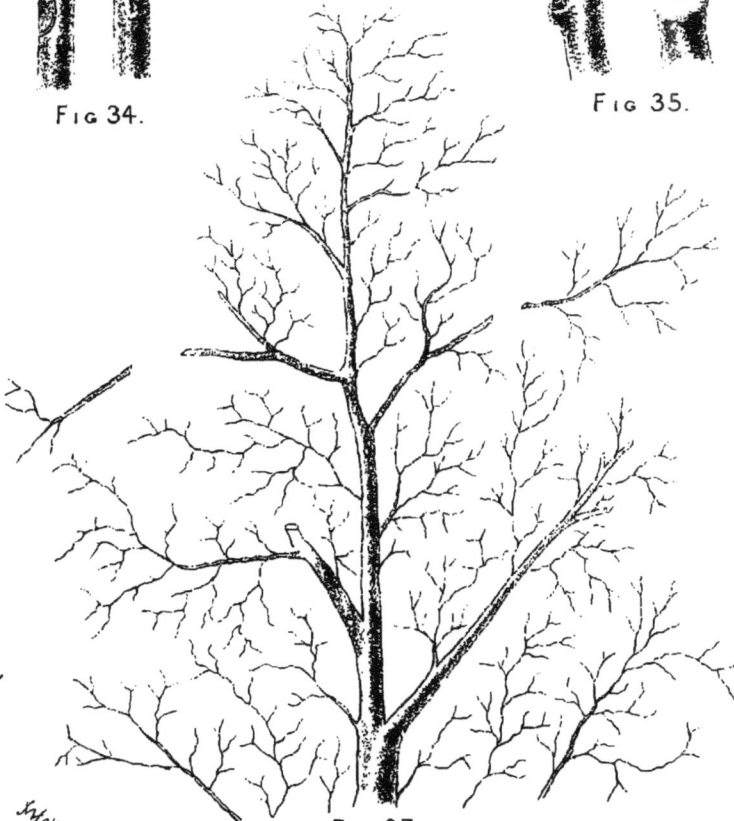

Fıg 37.

F ɪ ɢ 38.

F ɪ ɢ 40.

F ɪ ɢ 39.

F ɪ ɢ 41.

E SPILLER, LITH

CHAPTER XXIII.

Thinning Woods and Forests.

WHILE thick planting is absolutely necessary in order to ensure the timber produced being of a superior quality. it is, at the same time, equally as imperative to the successful accomplishment of this result that the plantations undergo a systematic and periodical course of thinnings. As *thin planting is highly objectionable* in a timber-point of view, so in a like manner, and to a like extent, is the over-crowding of the young trees. How desirable it is then that the forester should be thoroughly and practically acquainted with every detail in the proper management of forest trees. To the ignorance of certain matters, or to the negligence of their performance, I have often traced the failure of plantations. There is, perhaps, no operation connected with forestry which is less properly understood, and which is more generally neglected, than that of *thinning*. This I have found to be the case in different parts of the world.

The art of thinning may be described as the application of the knowledge of the habits, peculiarities, and physiological functions of trees, to a mass of forest or plantation, in such a manner that the proper amount of confinement will be given to the branches, combined with a well-regulated degree of room and air for the proper balance of health, all in such a manner that good, sound, and valuable timber will eventually be produced.

I shall now endeavor, therefore, to give afew practical hints on the subject, which I trust will be of some service to my readers.

There can be no rule laid down as to the proper distances apart at which trees should stand one from another at the various stages of their growth. There are no two plantations ever alike in their rate of growth. So much depends upon soil, situation, and aspect, as to whether the growth may be rapid or slow, that of two plantations planted at the same time, but in different parts of the country, one might require thinning when five years of age, while the other could very well do without this until it were ten years old. This is a fact which is well known to practical foresters, and one which I cannot too strongly impress upon my readers.

Without reference to the ages of the trees, I have often found the following rules applicable to the thinning of plantations under the various conditions which shall be named.

In plantations where the trees are grown purely for the purpose of producing superior timber without reference to shelter to lands beyond, the trees, when they attain a fair size, ought to stand at about one-fourth of their height one from another;—that is, supposing the trees are forty feet in height, they should then be standing ten feet apart. This rule applies chiefly to the *Coniferæ* and *Eucalypti;* and, in the case of deciduous trees, these should stand a little wider apart.

Where plantations are reared with the view of producing shelter and a second-rate quality of timber at maturity, the trees should be allowed a little more light and air. With these objects in view, therefore, the trees should stand at about one-third of their height from one another.

While the allowing trees in a plantation to get into an overcrowded condition is highly objectionable, and by all means to be avoided by the grower of good timber, this is not nearly so reprehensible or so injurious to the young crop as sudden and severe thinning. Of course, both cases are thoroughly opposed to sound forestry, still, in the former one a fair crop may still be obtained by careful thinning; but in that of the latter, the change from the warm crowded and protected condition, into that of a rush of light and air, is so great that the natural flow of the sap is disarranged to such an extent that disease sets in and general failure is often the result. Besides, should the trees survive such treatment, many are sure to be blown over with the winds from the roots not being sufficiently strong to support the plants.

It is, therefore, a very important point in the management of plantations not to allow them to become overcrowded.

The first indication that a plantation is in want of thinning, is when the young trees show that they are beginning to interfere with one another too much. I find it necessary to use the somewhat ambiguous mode of expression *too much*, as the interference of the trees with one another's branches, to a certain extent, is necessary in a plantation, in order that these lateral growths may be confined to such an extent only as will allow of their continuance on the trees to serve their proper purpose of elaborating the sap and causing increased growth of woody matter, without interfering with the proper development and expansion of the stem. The lower branches must, therefore, be confined and kept alive for a time until a succession of others come on, which will, of course, be the case as the trees grow upwards. What is required in thinning, therefore, is to watch that the trees are confined to just that particular degree which will prevent the branches interfering with the proper growth of the stem of the tree, and no more. If overcrowding is allowed in a plantation, the branches die off too soon, and the trees rush upwards for food and light, thus making length of stem, but not proportionate girth. An observant man can always tell when the difference between the two stages referred to begins.

In thinning, never attempt to keep the trees left standing at exactly the same distance apart one from the other, over the whole ground. It will be found in all plantations, that some trees require more room to develop themselves than others of the same species on perhaps the same piece of ground; and in order to give such trees a fair chance to come on, more relief may be necessary to them than is required by the others.   This would, of course, necessitate the former being left at greater distances from their neighbors in the plantation than the latter; consequently this would break up the general uniformity, supposing the trees were at first planted at regular distances apart.

One of the best rules to go by in thinning plantations is, to gradually take out the more inferior and least healthy plants, and to leave only the healthiest, strongest, and largest specimens to come on as the permanent crop—removing such inferior ones from time to time only as may be required to prevent over-crowding and to keep the plantation in a healthy condition generally.

Thinning should be done gradually, and as far as possible periodically—say, every three or four years, until the trees stand at from 16ft. to 20ft. apart, when those remaining will have attained that shape and growth which will permit them remaining until their period of maturity.

The operation of thinning should, in this country, be done in the winter time with deciduous trees, and in the autumn for such trees as the eucalypti, pines, and evergreens generally.

CHAPTER XXIV.

The Growing of Hedge Fences on our Agricultural Areas.

THE land-holders of this colony do not yet seem to understand the great increase in value which the cultivation of hedges is calculated to effect on their farms. At least we are entitled to judge of them in this light from the general absence of this description of fence on their properties. In travelling through even the most highly cultivated parts of the country, we meet with few hedges of any sort; the principal fence in most cases being of posts and wire, which give, generally speaking, a bare, cold, and unclothed aspect to lands naturally fertile.

But the absence of hedges does not give an unclothed look only to the cultivated lands of these countries. This state of things amounts to a present real disadvantage and loss in the cultivation of the lands, and therefore should be remedied as early as possible. The advantages of hedges round cultivated fields are chiefly the shelter and shade they afford to crops and live stock at all seasons of the year, but more especially in this country during the hot winds of summer and the cold winds of early spring, both of which affect stock and vegetation detrimentally. It is now a well understood fact that in fields surrounded by good hedges, grass and other crops are found at least two weeks earlier in spring than they are in fields without such protection; simply from the cause that the presence of hedges sifts the cold winds, thus lessening their force, and maintaining a degree of warmth not to be found in fields surrounded by post-and-wire fences. And for these reasons I have strongly to recommend the landed proprietors of this country to plant and cultivate hedges on their properties, as by doing so they will certainly vastly increase their value, both for the present and future.

I need not here enter into much detail in regard to the several modes of growing hedges, as were I to do so I should go much beyond the limits which I have laid down for myself in writing this work. I may, however, first state in a general way that hedges are, as a rule, easily cultivated, and may be reared on all descriptions of land, by simply attending to use plants adapted to the nature of the soil on which it is intended to rear them.

Before detailing the different kinds of plants which are suitable for hedges in this country, I shall first of all give a few general remarks on the subject of the management of hedges, which will apply to all, more or less, of the kinds to be named.

In all cases, the ground on the line where a hedge is planted should be clean and thoroughly free from stagnant water in the subsoil. It should be also trenched at least 18in. in depth, and from 2ft. to 3ft. in breadth, if practicable. In this trenching, all stones and other rubbish should be carefully removed. If the soil be somewhat poor in places, this should be made good by an intermixture of some other kind of a richer character, so as to make the whole of it in the line of fence as equable in quality as possible, and thus uniformity of growth in the plants composing the hedge will be secured.

This done, the surface of the ground should then be carefully levelled and well-pressed down along the immediate line where the plants are to be inserted, so that a good straight line may be cut for the laying-in of them.

The plants used in the laying down of a hedge should be of a strong, well-grown kind, with plenty of fibrous roots; and they should be carefully planted with all their roots spread well out to their full length, and the soil nicely moulded down and put regularly about them. Tramp the soil down only after the hole has been all filled up. The plants may be put in at distances ranging from 6in. to 10in. apart, in accordance with the nature of the plant and the character of the soil in which it is to be planted. These particulars I give in Chapter XXXIV. of this work.

The sowing of the seed in the line of fence is recommended in some cases instead of putting in the plants. Such plants as are suitable for this system of treatment are mentioned in the chapter just referred to. In this case the ground should be prepared in the manner above described, and after the surface of the ground has been thoroughly raked fine, the seed should be put in to a regular depth, and with about one or two seeds to every 3in. In sowing seeds in this way, great care should be exercised to see that the very best of articles only is used, as much disappointment will be the result if seed of an inferior quality be sown. Should the seed have been good and the plants come up pretty thickly, they should be thinned out after they have reached a height of from 3in. to 6in. In performing this operation, the plants left on the ground ought to stand as regularly as possible apart, although a weakly plant should not be left instead of a strong one in order simply to keep up uniformity of distance apart—that is, it will be much better to pull up a weakly plant which stands at the required distance apart, and leave a strong one 2in. or 3in. further on. This thinning should be carefully performed by one accustomed to such work, and all care taken to avoid disturbing the roots of the plants which are left to form the hedge.

If stock be kept in the fields adjoining, it will be necessary to protect the hedge with a fence on each side of it for a few years, until it has arrived at that stage when it will be beyond risk of destruction by stock. These fences should not be closer to the plants than about 4ft. In Fig. 42 I give an end view of a hedge so treated.

The young plants should be carefully attended to in the way of keeping them free of weeds, and stirring the soil round their stems for a breadth of at least 18in. on each side of the line.   Attention of this kind will more than repay the trouble and expense put upon them, by fewer failures and greater and vigorous growths.

Hedges should be planted about the end of June or beginning of July.   With the seed-sowing, the sooner in the rainy season this is done the better will the result be.

All hedges should be cut down and trained for a few years in order to encourage density, strength, and uniformity.   I generally make the first cutting in the autumn following the planting, and this to about 9in. or 10in. from the ground (Fig. 43).   Then, in the autumn of the next year, I again cut and trim up to about 15in. or 20in. above the surface (Figs. 44 and 45), and so on from year to year until the hedge is to the required height and shape.   In performing this cutting, care must be taken to encourage *lateral* growth and strength, as much as that of upright habit.

A good tool for cutting hedges is that known as the "hedge-bill" (see Fig. 46), which is in general use in Europe for this purpose.

Hedges may be cut and trained to almost any required form.   In Figs. 47, 48, and 49, I give a few of the generally-recognised shapes to which they are trained.

Now as to the kinds of hedge-plants suitable for cultivation in this colony.   This is a very difficult subject to deal with, and it has been before the public in the press over and over again, but without any satisfactory conclusion as to what is really a good hedge plant.   I don't speak of a purely ornamental evergreen hedge suitable for an enclosure to a gentleman's park or garden, but one that would be essentially, and in every respect, suitable for farms or fields.   The prince of hedge plants is the White Thorn, when it has a suitable soil and climate; but it will not answer in this dry and hot country.   It is true that there are some beautiful hedges of it in the cooler and more elevated parts of the colony, particularly at Mount Gambier and in the Mount Lofty hills, and these are as fine specimens of hawthorn hedges as may be seen in the old country; but they cannot be grown on the plains.   Various plants have been brought prominently before the public from time to time.   *Maclura auranliaca* (osage orange) was spoken very highly of in Victoria, and quantities of seed were sown here as an experiment; but, unless in very rich and special sites, it has been a failure here.   Then we have been hearing a great deal about the *Lycium horridum* – kaffir thorn ; but of this nothing definite can be yet said, although, so far, it is satisfactory.   A species of *Gleditschia* was highly extolled some years ago as a good hedge plant, but after a few trials it was given up.   The Gorse is extensively used in the Gumeracha and Mount Pleasant districts, and in other parts of the colony where the climate is cool; and when kept cut it makes a splendid fence ; but, unfortunately, it is too frequently left untouched, and the consequences are that it spreads out its branches laterally to such an extent that the chain roads in the above districts give scarcely room enough for vehicles to pass along.   And this is not the least evil.   The seeds are annually produced in large quantities, and are jerked out of the pods to a great distance, and then lie in the

Fıɢ 42.

Fıɢ 43.

Fıɢ 44.

Fıɢ 45.

Fıɢ 47.

Fıɢ 48.

Fıɢ 49.

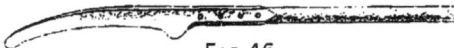

Fıɢ 46.

E. SPILLER. LITH

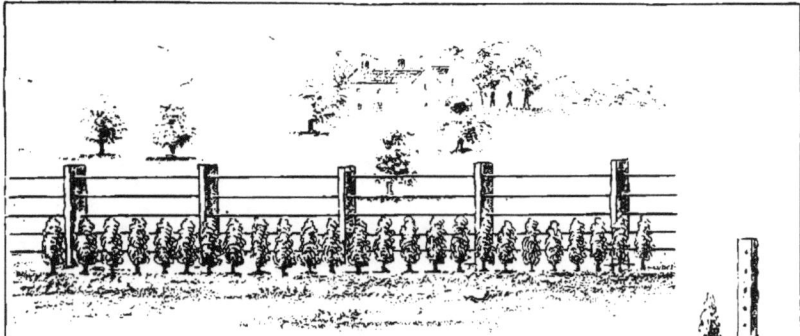

F IG 50.

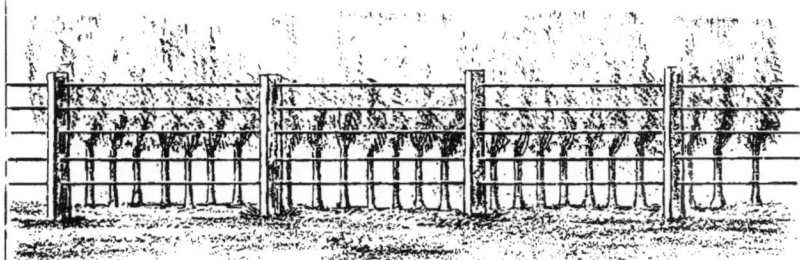

F IG 51.

F IG 52

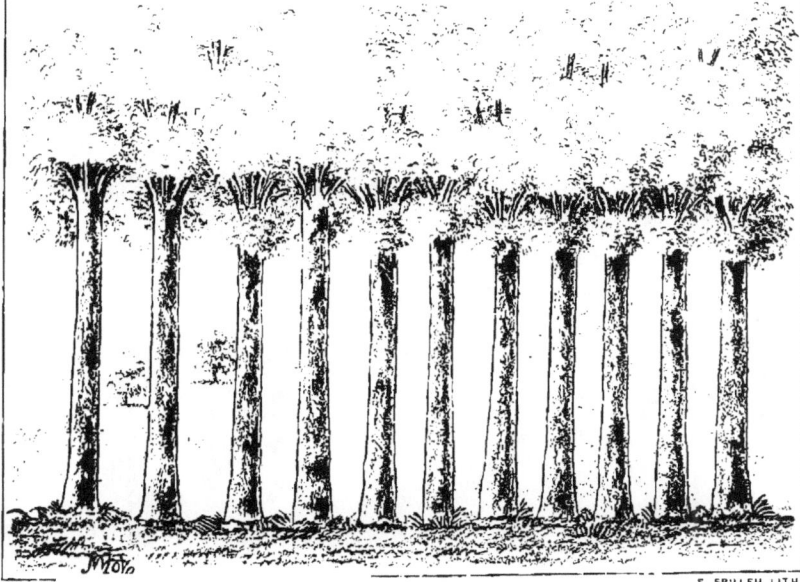

E. SPILLEH, LITH

ground, awaiting the first favorable condition of the soil—as after a fire, or when the land containing them is ploughed—to spring up in countless thousands, which entails an amount of labor to clear them of more value than the freehold of the land. The Sweetbriar makes a splendid fence when properly pruned, but if left uncut the seed-pods are regularly eaten by cattle in the dry weather, and as the seed passes through them, with its germinating powers undiminished, the fields and pastures get quickly covered with the briars, and these become a nuisance quite as formidable as the Gorse. The Olive is also a good hedge plant, and if properly attended to makes a useful fence. It grows on the poorest of soil. The Kangaroo Island *acacia* is, after all, our most useful hedge plant, as it will grow without trouble in any kind of soil and in any part of the colony, and when well-kept is highly ornamental. The greatest objection to it is its liability to destruction by bush fires; yet, after witnessing all that may be said for and against it, there is not anything better as a generally useful hedge plant.

Of the plants named (leaving out the *Lycium*, which is yet only upon trial) these may be classed as follows:—The Kangaroo Island Acacia for general utility stands first, the Sweet Briar second, the Gorse third, and the Hawthorn and Olive fourth in order of utility for general cultivation.

I am of opinion that, in some districts of the colony, a very serviceable farmers' hedge could be grown of the Lombardy Poplar, as is done in some districts of France and Italy. These trees are planted thickly together in the line of fence—say at distances ranging from 18in. to 24in. apart, according to taste, and kept regularly pruned and lopped in such a way that in a few years a close and impenetrable hedge is the result. The trees are thinned as they become too thick, and timber is thus provided for the use of the farm. The system works well in Europe, and I do not see why it should not do equally so in some parts of this country as well. In Figs. 50 and 51 are shown the young poplars when newly planted out. Fig. 52 represents them pruned and lopped at 3-4 years of age; and in Fig. 53 I have tried to give an idea of the hedge as it stands completed at say 6-8 years of age. Some of our more hardy *Eucalypti*—such as the Redgum, Tasmanian bluegum, and South Australian bluegum—would do equally as well, if not better, than the Poplar. A fence of this kind could be easily kept, and would give much more shelter to the fields beyond than the ordinary hedge plants would do.

CHAPTER XXV.

Selecting Plants from the Public Nurseries.

I will now endeavor to give a few practical hints on some matters which ought to be observed in the selection of plants from the public nurseries in the colony.

As the operation of planting is somewhat expensive in this country, it is particularly necessary that every precaution be taken to ensure success the first season, so that little or no filling-up planting in after years will be required. A very great means towards this most desirable end is, therefore, the taking care to plant good strong healthy plants only. Of every hundred persons who plant in the colony, perhaps a proportion of something like ninety get their plants from our public nurseries. It is very important, then, that our nurserymen should sell the very best of stock only.

The first thing to consider, when about to purchase trees, should be—Which nursery in the colony comes nearest in soil, situation, aspect, and elevation to the site you are about to plant? Having found this, then I would say, buy your trees there. This is a very important matter indeed, and ought never to be overlooked. At the present time it is never thought of, and hence no doubt bad results arise. What I mean to impress upon my readers in this paragraph is, that for *healthy* and generally satisfactory plantations the trees put out should, as far as possible, be *reared* in a soil and climate somewhat analogous to those of the site of the plantation. At least there ought never to be a very marked difference in these. Hence one very important point in favor of everyone growing their own plants. For instance, how absurd it would it be to plant a piece of poor sandy soil in a high-lying exposed country, with plants reared in a low-lying warm gully, where the soil is a deep black, rich loam, and the situation nicely sheltered from all storms and cold winds. This is apparent, and no further explanation is necessary.

Plants reared in poor soils are always the best, and can be transplanted out into almost any kind of site, even into one at a high elevation.

For the formation of plantations in exposed situations, choose plants of a strong, bushy, and generally healthy appearance. Allow no pruning of the trees before they leave the nursery, nor until after the first year from date of planting.

All open-root plants should have plenty of fibrous roots, and in the case of the slower-growing kinds, they should be transplanted *once* in the nursery lines before they are put out into the plantations. If, however, they are only required for lining out in the nursery at home, then, of course, one-year seedlings will be sufficient for this purpose.

Great care is necessary in the selection of plants in pots. The following are some of the principal points to be attended to in their purchase : —Avoid such as are drawn up and spindley. A very large proportion of potted plants are of this character; I have seen plants in a 4in. pot stand 30in. high, with their foliage of a pale, yellow-green colour, showing disease and general weakness. Still, it must be admitted that trees of this class are planted and yet do well. It would be unwise, however, to conclude from this that spindley trees are the proper kind to purchase. No man knowing anything at all about the physiology of plants would suppose so for one moment. They, of course, succeed at times by great care and attention in staking, watering, &c., combined with the excellent character of the climate, which does much to push forward the tenderly-grown plant into full life and renewed action, even under most disadvantageous circumstances.

Pines are often kept in small 4in. pots for two, and even sometimes three years. These are really not worth planting, and should, in my opinion, be burned as worthless stock ; at all events, let me strongly advise my readers to avoid purchasing them.

Pines and gums should not be longer than nine or ten months in the pots, and at the time of planting they ought not to be over 8in. or 12in. in height, and they should be wide-spreading and branchy, and have been reared the greater portion of the time in the open air and not under cover, as is too frequently done.

Some nurserymen have a habit of "*trimming*," as it is called, all deciduous trees as they are sent out of the nursery. This operation is carried out upon the roots of the plants as well as their side branches. The system is iniquitous, and cannot be too strongly condemned. As already explained under another heading of this work, such lateral shoots of the branches as show signs of interfering with the growth of the proper leader, should be *shortened* only before the plants leave the nursery; but, as for trimming up the roots, do it not at all, unless it be occasionally the shortening of a very strong tap-root, which may be devoid of fibrous roots, and therefore better cut off in order to encourage a flow of rootlets from the edges of the cut—which generally follows an operation of this kind.

CHAPTER XXVI.

The Different Methods of Rearing Young Trees in the Nursery.

ALTHOUGH, I daresay, the greater proportion of my readers will prefer to purchase their ʃplants from the public nurserymen rather than go to the trouble of rearing these themselves, still there will be a few who will reverse this condition of things; and for such I will now endeavor to give a brief description as to how a small nursery should be established, and trees reared in it under the different systems of culture now in vogue in the colony.

The advantages arising from having small home nurseries cannot be too highly estimated. When extensive planting is carried out, I do not know of any country in which these would be of more advantage and produce better results than this. The climate of our country is so dry that trees cannot be safely carried any great distance without bad results arising to them ; besides, trees reared in the neighborhood of the site which they are to occupy permanently, are much more valuable and more likely to succeed upon it than if they were grown some hundreds of miles away, in an entirely different altitude, and with different surroundings. As a rule, however, I advocate farmers getting their plants from the public nurseries.

In almost every farmer's garden a suitable spot can be selected for a small nursery, and with a very little expense such appliances can always be erected upon it as will enable him to grow all the young trees he may require for planting upon his holding. Such a site as I refer to should, as far as possible, be somewhat sheltered, and have a soil of a free loamy nature. This should be well and regularly trenched to a depth of at least 24in., specially fenced off by wire netting and paling, (in order to prevent the inroads of poultry), and afterwards laid out systematically with footpaths, and divided into equal-sized blocks. It is also an advantage to enclose the ground with a quick-growing hedge for shelter.

On the north side of the ground thus laid off as a nursery, a Propagating Shed should be erected ; this to be of such a size as the requirements of the planter will necessitate. The structure may consist of split palings saplings, or "bamboo" reeds. The side facing the north should be

Fig 54.

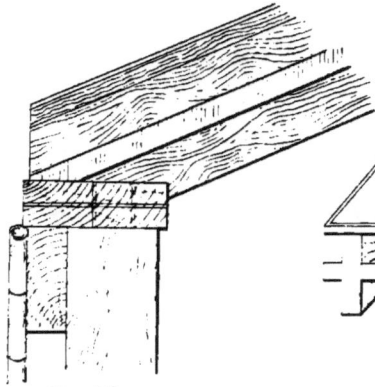

Fig 55.

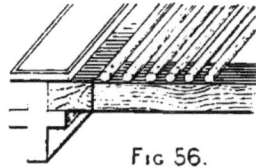

Fig 56.

Fig 57.

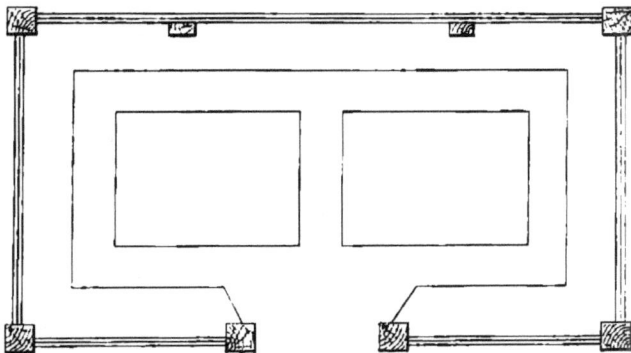

Fig 58.

close fitting, in order to thoroughly protect the plants, which will be placed inside, from the hot winds coming from that direction.   The top should consist of sliding shades, made of deal framework, with bamboo reeds nailed lengthways to it.   These shades must be made portable, in order that they can be removed at will, and thus prevent the drawing up of the young plants, which, as I have already pointed out, is very objectionable in the rearing of forest trees of any kind.

Fig. 57 represents a Propagating Shed of the kind referred to ;

Figs. 54, 55, and 56 show the mechanism of sliding frames for the top ; and

Fig. 58 the ground-plan of the shed.

A building of this kind is indispensable for the rearing of plants in a climate such as ours, and may be used for potting plants, and for the storage of such as may be of a somewhat tender nature.

I shall now endeavor to give some general directions in regard to the rearing of young trees.   There are three ways of doing this, namely, (1) open root in the nursery-beds ; (2) in pots : and (3) in bamboo reeds. Each of these systems has its special features and recommendations, and I propose, then, to describe the *modus operandi* of each separately, and at the same time to indicate the particular kinds of trees which are best reared under each one.   I begin with that of—

Plants Grown Open-Root.

Briefly described, this consists of growing the plants in the open ground, without reference to any artificial aid for keeping the soil about their roots during the process of transplanting. This is the system in universal application in Europe and America, and it is there found to be admirably adapted to the rearing of all kinds of plants, both evergreens and deciduous.   Here, however, the system cannot have such general application as in more cold countries, owing to the quiescent stage of the growth of trees in this climate being uncertain in its duration and season, and also from the intensely drying nature of the air, to which it is at times dangerous to expose the tender roots of trees. Owing to the comparative mildness of the climate here all the year round, our evergreen trees, both indigenous and exotic kinds, do not seem to have any clearly defined period for ripening their young wood, and as these kinds of trees, if grown under the system of "open root," must only be lifted when their growth is quiescent, the difficulty of applying it to trees of this class is at once apparent. Of course it can be done, and that successfully, as has been shown upon the Forest Reserves ; but without some good practical knowledge of plant physiology applied to the system, it is unsafe to extend it to planting generally in this country. The great point in transplanting evergreens which have been reared in this way, is to watch for the dormant season of their growth, and to plant them out in dull damp weather only, with their roots well puddled in earth and water.   By attention to these matters of detail, good results can always be obtained by the system here.

The principal features in favor of open-root rearing of plants, where it can be safely done, is that stronger, better-rooted, and much more healthy plants can be reared by it than by any other system. Frequent transplanting in the nursery lines induces the formation of a mass of fibrous roots, which will materially assist the plant in establishing itself on its new site in the plantation.

Owing, however, to the difficulties attending it which I have just pointed out, I do not recommend its adoption by our farmers to the evergreen class of plants.

To all deciduous trees, however, the system should be universally applied. The seedlings may be grown thickly in boxes, or in open beds, according to the degree of hardiness of the tree, and transplanted out in the nursery during the rainy season—say in July or August. The plants should be put in at from 3in. to 8in. apart in the rows, according to their character and likelihood or otherwise to make good growths during the year. The rows should be from 10in. to 18in. apart, being lessened or increased in accordance with the same rule. Room must always be given to the trees to make good strong stems, well covered with leaves and branchlets, and also to allow the soil about them being regularly hoed and all weeds kept under. Frequent hoeing during the summer time will encourage their growth and prevent unhealthiness arising from their closeness to one another.

In " lining out" or planting the young trees in this way, the operation should be conducted as follows:—The soil dug up and levelled, gently beat it down with the spade, and then stretch a garden line across the whole length of the block intended to be filled with the trees ; this done, then make a cutting in the earth, along the said line, to the depth required by the length of the roots of the seedlings. This cutting should be nearly perpendicular, and as regular as possible. Remove the plants carefully from the seed-bed, and " puddle" their roots at once; then lay them along the cut line, putting each one in separately and covering up the roots by the hand with as much soil as will keep the plants in position and prevent the roots from drying. The line all finished, dig the soil over the roots of the trees ; tramp firmly with the feet, then make up the space until it is a little broader than the required distance between the rows of plants; level and press with the spade, and cut edge as formerly ; proceed with laying in the plants, and so on from row to row, until the required number of plants are put in, all as represented in Fig. 59.

Cuttings of trees should be lined out in much the same manner as described above. They should be cut from good strong young wood, of one or two years' growth, from 9in. to 12.in in length, somewhat rounded at bottom and the top cut sharply upward, at an acute angle immediately above the bud in the wood (Fig. 60), and planted in the ground with the soil well-up to the bud, as shown in Figs. 60 and 61. In Fig. 62 I show the young tree beginning to form upon the cutting. When trees reared from cuttings are planted out into the plantations, they should be inserted in the ground in such a way that the whole of the cutting, and about an inch of the shoot, is buried in the soil—see Fig. 63. This is necessary for the proper support of the shoot.

FIG 59.

FIG 60.

FIG 61

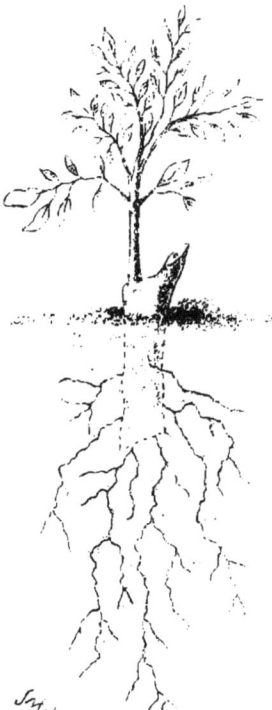

FIG 62

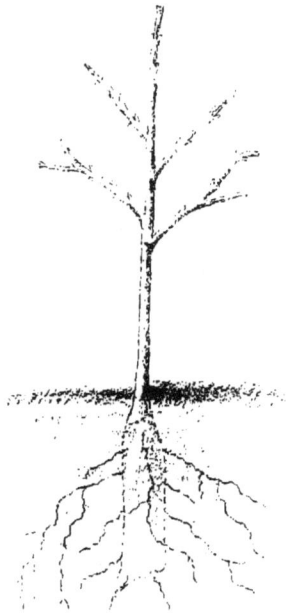

FIG 63.

E. SPILLER LITH

Plants Reared in Pots.

This method of raising plants consists, as is well known, in growing them in earthenware pots instead of openly in the nursery ground. The method possesses many good points, while at the same time there are also several objections to its application to forestry under all circumstances.

The special features in its favor are these:—All roots are carefully preserved; the plant can be moved from place to place to harden and thus made gradually suitable for exposed planting; and it can be transplanted at any season of the year, and in almost any weather, without feeling injurious effects therefrom. These are very valuable properties in favor of the system.

The disadvantages of the system to the proper growth of forest trees are:—Should the plant be kept long in the pot, its roots get what is termed pot-bound: that is, the roots assume such a coil-like shape that no amount of after culture will remedy this; and when the tree is planted they take a purely downward tendency, without extending themselves horizontally (which is their natural habit); thus they soon get down into the cold subsoil, and the tree often becomes stunted and unhealthy in consequence. Again, it is well known that trees which have stood long in pots, with the roots contracted in the manner described, are not able to support themselves properly in the ground, and often get blown down with ordinary winds when they attain to tree size. Be advised then, never to plant a young tree which has been long confined in a small pot.

Owing to the nature of our climate making the quiescent period of *evergreen* trees somewhat uncertain, as has already been referred to in this chapter, the system of rearing plants in pots is peculiarly well adapted to trees of this class. To the ordinary run of farmers, plants in pots are much more suitable for their planting than those grown in any other way, because (1) they are less liable to injury from neglect previous to planting; and (2) they will bear *bad planting* better than open-root plants will do. At present, the only real drawback to their general adoption is their price, which, from the present limited demand, is higher than any farmer can afford to pay in the formation of a plantation of a few thousands of trees. This, however, will right itself as the demand for plants increases, and their sale upon a large scale will allow our spirited nurserymen to accept smaller profits.

The pots used should not be less than those quoted as " 4in.," that is, having a diameter of 4in. inside at the top. Any size above this is, of course, preferable, and should be used if possible. Sizes 4½in. and 5in. are very suitable for all practical purposes. These cost from £5 to £6 per thousand. Plants for potting should be reared in small boxes; brandy cases are very suitable for the purpose (Fig. 65). The process of " potting " should, if possible, be done in nice cool cloudy weather, and with soil of a fine sharp sandy-loam nature. The seeds may be sown in the boxes about March or April for transplanting into the pots in August or September; or they may be sown in September or October for potting in January. The plants will then remain some six or seven months only in the pots before they are put out into the plantation. Immediately the plants are potted they should be put under a frame made entirely of calico, or one of stonework with glass frame on top (Fig. 64), in the ordinary way, and kept nice and moist for some eight or ten days, until their roots have " struck " once more. This can be judged by the appearance of the plants : if all right, they will stand upright and have no appearance of drooping. After the plants are considered secure in this way, they should be removed from the frame and "plunged" in the propagating shed. This plunging consists of packing the pots close together in nice loose sandy soil to their full depth, but closer than is shown in Fig 66, in which position they should now remain until the summer months are over. It is as well to have beds specially prepared with concrete floors for this plunging, in order to prevent worms getting amongst the roots of the plants. Once every fortnight, or three weeks, the pots should be gently lifted and replaced in their positions again, so as to check any undue growth of the roots through the holes in their bottoms.

Plants Grown in Bamboo Tubes.

In the Forest Department of India, a system of rearing young plants in short pieces of bamboo cane, was introduced a good many years ago by a Captain Beddome, one of the conservators of forests there. This was found to be admirably suited for the purpose, and is thus briefly described in the *Journal of Forestry* for July, 1880 :—" Cut the bamboo of which estate baskets are made, and which is not more than an inch or two in circumference, into bits about three inches long. Place these pieces endways close together, in thousands, cover over with forest mould or fine soil and sow your seed. In this way there will be from one to three or four seedlings in each piece of bamboo. When carried out in the bits of bamboo the best plant can be left, the others being removed and utilised immediately or at a subsequent period."

When the subject of forest conservancy was first being mooted in this colony, His Excellency Sir Anthony Musgrave, the then Governor of South Australia, in a lecture on the subject, incidentally referred to Captain Beddome's system, which he had heard of or seen carried into effect in India. The idea of trying to adopt the method to tree planting here was not, so far as I am aware, suggested at the meeting in question; simply, I would suppose, from the want of bamboos wherewith to carry it into effect. The idea, however, occurred to Mr. Murray, who was subsequently appointed as conservator to the Forest Board, that the same results might be obtained by the use of small pieces of the well-known reed, *arundo donax*. Acting upon this notion, he had several pieces prepared, filled with fine soil, and gum seeds sown in them; and the result was such that on his appointment to the Forest Board he suggested that he might be allowed to apply the system to the planting on the Bundaleer Reserve, where the Board had just commenced operations. This the Board allowed, and under the immediate supervision of Mr. John Curnow, nurseryman, the system has been carried out at Bunda-

Fɪɢ 64

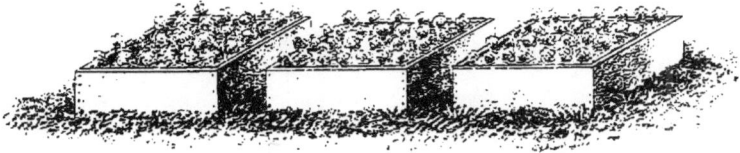

Fɪɢ 65.

Fɪɢ 66.

E SPILLER LITH

leer with a certain degree of success in the raising and planting of *eucalyptus* plants.   With pines it has proved a failure.

I will now describe the system.

The reed referred to *(arundo donax)* is a native of the south of Europe, and is now seen growing luxuriantly in different parts of the colony.   It can be cultivated here wherever there is moisture in the subsoil, although, of course, it prefers deep, moist, low-lying spots for quick and rapid growth.   The roots (or cuttings) should be planted during the winter season, and may be planted in rows 3 to 4ft. apart. The ground should be cultivated about them occasionally, so as to encourage health and vigorous growth.   The first year's shoots will generally be found too small and slender for the purpose of forest-tree growing ; they should, therefore, be cut down two or three times during the season and removed.   It should be remembered that the oftener the reeds are cut, the stronger will the growths become.

The second year's growths will generally be found suitable for the purpose of tree-rearing, and if the reeds have been planted in a congenial site, sometimes more than two cuttings may be obtained from the same stocks in one season.   The young and tender growths should now therefore be cut and stacked for a time until their woody matter has dried and become slightly hardened, after which they may be cut into the required lengths.

All tubes should be cut and rotted twelve months before being used. This was not done at first, with the result that many plants died off from the reed not decaying in time to allow the full expansion of the stem.

The operation of cutting the tubes should be done with a sharp saw, and the motive power may be by horse, water, or hand, in accordance with the number of tubes required.   In the Forest Department Nurseries the work is performed by water-power chiefly.   For all ordinary purposes, however, a very sharp small hand-saw will suffice.

The tubes should be cut to about 5in. in length, and it is necessary for the proper working of them afterwards, that they be all as nearly equal in length as possible.   When cutting them, the knots or junctions of the various growths should be left out as much as practicable, as shown in Fig. 71.

Should reeds be scarce, however, these junctions may be utilised, and the woody matter afterwards cleared from within them by a long angular shaped tool such as is represented in Fig. 70, before they are made use of.

The next operation consists in laying the tubes in position for the reception of the soil and seeds.   There may be various ways of doing this according to the conveniences and appliances of the intending planter, but we have found the following to be a ready and inexpensive way of doing it :—Beds about 4ft. broad, 9in. deep, and of such lengths as may be required, are laid out in the nursery ground, with sides and bottoms of concrete or boards.   These bottoms must be properly level in order to secure uniformity of surface on the top of the bamboos.   An inch or two of good loamy soil should now be spread upon the bottom of the bed, and the tubes then taken one by one and packed tightly together as shown in Fig. 67. This should be followed throughout until the bed is full; then afterwards (with a levelling tool, as shown in Fig. 69) the tops of the tubes should be gently pressed down until a level surface is obtained.

Fine sharp forest-mould, having been previously kept perfectly dry, should now be filled into the bamboos in the following way:—With a sieve a man gently riddles the soil over the top of the tubes, while another man, with a strong piece of wood (Fig. 68) beats their tops until the soil is all shaken down into them. Great care must always be taken to see that the tubes are perfectly full of soil, otherwise bad results are sure to follow.

The very best of seed having been procured, this should now be sown, by putting two or three seeds in each tube; afterwards, soil of the description already given should be riddled equally over the whole of the bed to a depth of somewhat less than half an inch and until the tops of the tubes are completely covered.

Immediately after the sowing of the seed is completed, the whole of the bed should receive a good watering applied gently with a very fine hose. This watering should be repeated at least once a day (in the evening).

The bed should now be protected during the day time by shades constructed of bamboos or palings, as may be found most convenient, and erected some 6ft. from the ground on posts placed 8ft. apart along the edges of the beds.

In rainy weather remove the shadings, as these will cause a "drip" which will lift the soil and seeds out of the tubes. Indeed, until the seeds have germinated and the plants are secure in their tubes, care must be taken to see that the rain itself when heavy does not touch the beds, as the same result will follow. During heavy rains, a tarpaulin or piece of calico can be stretched over the beds for their protection.

After the seeds have germinated, they should be carefully looked to, by watering in the evening and shading during dry and hot weather. In cool weather, however, all shades may be removed with advantage.

When the plants have reached a height of half an inch or so (which should be regulated to take place about March or April) the process of sorting, thinning, checking, and hardening the plants will now take place. This consists in taking out the tubes with the hands, removing all superfluous seedlings, leaving one strong plant only in each tube, and afterwards packing them away close together in another concrete bed, but on a higher and drier site if possible. The plants will now grow slowly, and will thus become fine handy subjects for exposed planting by the month of July or August.

19

FIG 67.

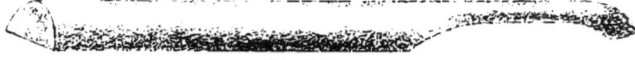

FIG 68.

FIG 70

FIG 69.

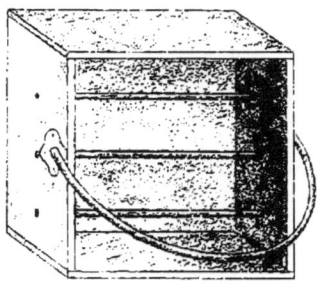

FIG 72.

FIG 73

FIG 71

FIG 77.

FIG 74

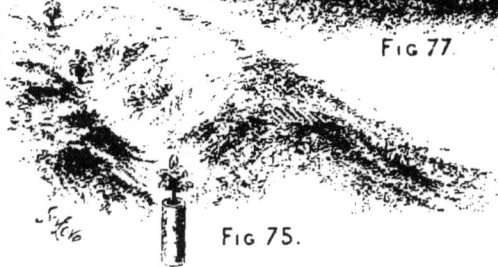

FIG 75.

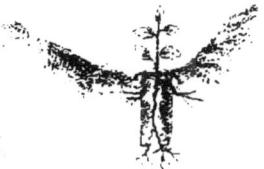

FIG 76

E. SMILLER, LITH

CHAPTER XXVII.

Trees Suitable for Cultivation in South Australia, with their Description, Soils upon which they Grow, Uses of Timber, and Mode of Culture.

THE capabilities of this colony in regard to the growth and profitable culture of exotic trees have not yet been clearly defined. The settlement of the country is of course of too recent a date for much to have been attempted in the introduction of trees from the forests of other parts of the world; yet more has been done in this way than may at the first glance appear. And while the work of introduction goes on apace each year, we have already such a number and variety of foreign species acclimatised as are sufficient to show us at least that our forests are capable of being permanently and profitably improved with these. So favorable are our soil and climate to some of the exotic trees that their annual growth with us is in several cases about three times greater than that which they attain in their natural state. Of course, this is where they have been planted in specially suitable spots.

The list which I am now about to give will embrace, besides those trees indigenous to the colony which are worth cultivation for their timber, only such exotics as are known to succeed well in our climate. While the list will deal chiefly with what are generally looked upon as forest trees, others, possessing ornamental attractions only, will also be included so as to make the work as comprehensively useful as possible. It must, however, at the same time be distinctly understood that the list is not a complete one as regards the trees suitable for ornamental planting in the colony, and that so far as trees of this class are embraced, it will deal only with such as are in most general request. The list will be taken up alphabetically, in accordance with the botanic names, and each tree will be briefly described and information given in regard to the soils and situations upon which it will grow, the economic uses of its timber, and the manner in which it should be propagated. In one or two cases a sketch showing a typical specimen will be given. Following out this course, I begin with :—

ACACIA DECURRENS.— *Willd.*

This is the well-known black wattle tree, which yields one of the tannic barks of commerce. According to Baron F. Von Mueller, the bark produces from 18 to 33 per cent. of tannic acid. The tree is a rapid grower, and is indigenous to the coast country extending from our south-east through Victoria, New South Wales, to Queensland; 30ft. to 50ft. in height ; timber soft, and not durable.

When young this is a very ornamental tree, afterwards it gets very straggling and rugged-looking.

Should be cultivated for its bark. Luxuriates in sandy soils; will grow well in limestone country, and in fact there are few sites upon which it will not grow.

Sow the seed in the ground where the tree is to stand.

ACACIA DEALBATA.—*Link.*

The silver wattle, common to the plain and hills about Adelaide. It is simply a variety of the former. The bark is less valuable than that of the other. Makes a good ornamental tree for a few years.

The remarks as to soil and culture given under *A. decurrens* are applicable to this tree as well.

ACACIA MELANOXYLON.—*R. Brown.*

(Blackwood.)

Indigenous to the cooler parts of our colony, and therefore well-known in the country. In the south-east attain heights of 50 to 60ft., and 3ft. in diameter. The timber is of excellent quality, being light, durable, and of good lateral strength, and is available for furniture-making.

The tree must have a cool moist bottom, with a loamy soil, to do well in.

Soak the seed in hot water, and sow in the plantation broadcast or in rows.

ACACIA PYCNANTHA.—*Bentham.*

(Broad-leaved Wattle.)

The great " mimosa " tree of commerce, and common to this colony and Victoria. The bark yields from 30 to 35 per cent. of the best tannic acid. Seldom attains a greater height than 20 to 24ft., grows rapidly, and may be cut for stripping purposes when five or six years of age. It springs up spontaneously in nearly all parts of the country, even after the land has been cropped for many years in succession.

I recommend its extensive culture on the poorer parts of our farms as a very remunerative crop. Seed can be collected almost anywhere. These should be well soaked in hot water (almost boiling) and sweated until quite soft, then sow at once. It is a good tree to rear as a "nurse" amongst more valuable kinds, or as break-winds and binders in drifting sands.

ACER PSEUDO-PLATANUS.—*Linné.*

(Sycamore, or False Maple.)

A well-known deciduous tree, indigenous to Europe. The timber is of good quality and suitable for implements, furniture, and turners' work. Grows to over 100ft. in height, and is recommended as an ornamental tree.

The tree does not stand the hot winds well in the colony, but in sheltered spots, with a fair amount of moisture, it may be planted with a fair chance of success.

Will grow on different kinds of soils—sandy, clayey, or loamy. Propagate from seeds; sow in rows, and transplant out into the nursery lines one year before putting out in the plantation.

AILANTHUS GLANDULOSA.—*Desf.*

(The Tree of Heaven.)

A broad-topped deciduous tree suitable for ornamental plantations and avenues. Indigenous to China, grows 20ft. to 30ft. in height and 12in. to 24in. in diameter. Very large leaves, unequally pinnate, with long footstalks, and numerous flowers in a terminating pedicle. Wood hard, heavy, glossy like satin, and susceptible of a fine polish. (Loudon.)

A rapid grower. Does well on any soil, and will grow on very poor ones. Suitable for planting on limestone or other calcareous soils.

Propagate from cuttings of the roots, or by seeds sown in rows in the open nursery grounds.

ARAUCARIA EXCELSA.—*R. Brown.*

(Norfolk Island Pine.)

As the name indicates, we have here a tree native of Norfolk Island, and popularly known as the pine of that island. We read of its attaining a height of over 220ft., and 8–10ft. in diameter in that portion of the globe. For masts of ships and other purposes in connection with ship building, the timber is invaluable. (Mueller.)

The straight, well-proportioned appearance of this tree, with its radiating branches are now well known in this country, to the soil and climate of which it appears to adapt itself readily. In the many gardens in the neighborhood of Adelaide, some very fine specimens are now attaining good heights and diameters of stem.

The tree is very accommodating in regard to soil and situation. It will grow in soil having a limestone subsoil, but it will become prematurely aged if this is not broken through, so as to make passage for the roots. It, of course, thrives best in warm, sheltered situations, with good soil and plenty of percolating moisture; but in almost any situation the tree will make a strong effort to grow.

Propagate from seeds, which should be sown as soon as possible after they are collected.

ARAUCARIA CUNNINGHAMII.—*Aiton.*

(Moreton Bay Pine.)

From Moreton Bay, in Queensland. A peculiar tree with tufty branches, but withal a very ornamental species. According to Baron Mueller it attains a height of 130ft. The timber is of fair quality, and is used by cabinetmakers chiefly.

Already in general use for ornamental planting about Adelaide, where it succeeds to the best of expectation. There are some very fine specimens about our principal gardens, some of which are over 80ft. in height.

The tree delights in deep soil with good shelter, in which position it will grow rapidly and with every feature of health and strength. It will, however, also grow to good dimensions in somewhat exposed situations where the soil is even poor and calcareous.

Raise from seeds, which sow immediately after collecting.

ARAUCARIA BIDWILLII.—*Hooker.*

(The Bunya Bunya Tree.)

Queensland, between Brisbane and the Burnett River; grows 100 and 200ft. in height, and from 3ft. to 4ft. 8in. in diameter, (W. Hill.) There are extensive forests of the tree.

A large massive looking tree of great beauty. Trunk straight; smooth bark; branches in whorls like the spokes of a wheel.

The tree produces large cones 9in. to 12in. in length, and 10in. in diameter; seeds, 2in. to 2½in. long and 1in. broad, and largely used by the natives as food. Timber strong and good, with beautiful veins when polished. (W. Hill.)

Grows freely in this colony. A little more fastidious in regard to soil and situation than *A. excelsa*, but still a hardy tree here, and worthy of extensive planting in ornamental grounds.

Propagate from the seeds, and rear in pots.

ARAUCARIA COOKII.—*R. Brown.*

(Captain Cook's Pine.)

Indigenous to New Caledonia. A very large and beautiful tree, with great ornamental capabilities.

Propagate from seed. The tree grows well in our climate.

ARAUCARIA RULEI.—*Mueller.*

New Caledonia. Baron Mueller says it is a magnificent tree, with large shining foliage; doubtless not merely of decorative, but also of utilitarian value.

Grown from seeds.

CASUARINA QUADRIVALVIS.—*La Billardiere.*

(The Sheaoak.)

South Australia; height 20ft. to 30ft., with diameters of 18in. to 24in.; timber useful for axe-handles, wheel-spokes, furniture-making, fencing, and firewood.

This is a very handsome tree, and does well for planting in masses, to contrast with other kinds of trees in ornamental plantations.

It grows freely in soils of the poorest description, and is particularly useful for planting in limestone country and on the sea-coast.

Can readily be grown by simply sowing the seed in the plantation. When reared in the nursery the plants should be put in pots.

CEDRUS DEODARA.

(Indian Cedar.)

E. SPILLER LITH.

BIOTA ORIENTALIS.—*Don.*

(The Chinese Arborvitæ.)

China and Japan. Grows 20ft. high; forms a dense pyramidal bush of great beauty. Suitable only for well-sheltered ornamental grounds in this country. It delights in good, deep, sandy-loam soils.

CATALPA SPECIOSA.

(The Catalpa Tree.)

Indigenous to the middle states of America, where it forms a large tree of over 100ft. in height and from 3ft. to 4ft. in diameter at the base. It is of remarkable celerity of growth, almost equalling in that respect the *eucalyptus* family. The leaves are large and deciduous. The timber is very durable, and is now largely used for telegraph poles, railway sleepers, fence posts, and for machinery construction, The writer has a piece of timber in excellent preservation which had lain in the ground for some seventy-five years.

The tree is generally found on the banks of rivers, and in somewhat swampy places. I, however, find it to do well here in all spots where the soil is deep and the subsoil cool. Where the soil is deep, rich, and kept constantly moist by percolation, and the site somewhat sheltered, it grows very rapidly in this country. We have it in the Wirrabara Forest over 10ft. in height at eighteen months old. The tree has only lately been introduced to the forest reserves, and, so far, it shows to be a great success.

Propagate from seed—which should be sown in the spring, and the plants transplanted out into the nursery rows one season before putting out into the plantation.

CEDRUS DEODARA.—*London.*

(The Deodar, or Indian Cedar.)

On the Himalaya Mountains in India, at elevations ranging from 3,000ft. to 12,000ft. above the sea. In these regions we find it intermixed with *Abies Smithiana, Picea pindrow*, and *Pinus longifolia.*

A majestic and finely-proportioned tree. Foliage a light sparkling green. If allowed plenty of room, throws out great lateral branches, bending down and lying upon the ground. Sketch of young tree given on opposite side.

The timber is of a light yellow color, close grained, agreeably scented, light, extremely durable, well-resisting the vicissitudes of a variable climate, and furnishes one of the best building timbers known. Pillars of Kashmir Mosques of this wood are found sound after 400 years, and bridges of still greater antiquity are in existence. White ants hardly ever attack the heart wood. Boats built of this wood last forty years. It is also used extensively for canal edges and for railways. (Baron F. Von Mueller.)

The tree is not too particular as to the kind of soil in which it will grow. It will thrive in both light and strong soils; but these must

never lie on a retentive subsoil, or be in a wet spot. If they do, the
tree will die. Give it a deep soil, with plenty of moving moisture, and
a good result will follow.

Of course, from its natural habits, the tree likes a high elevation. Our
mountain ranges and gullies are well suited for its cultivation. There
are some very fine specimens now growing at Highercombe ; one of these
covers a space of over 60ft. in breadth.

Propagate from seed. Sow thinly in boxes and transplant into pots
in the way already directed.

CEDRUS LIBANI.—*Barrelier*.

(The Cedar of Lebanon.)

Mount Lebanon, in Syria ; 100ft. in height; grand and majestic ;
great spreading branches ; one of our best ornamental trees. See other
side.

Timber soft, reddish, very durable, and much used in ancient times
in the building of mosques, &c.

Will grow in almost any kind of soil so long as it is deep, open, and
free from retentiveness below. It must, however, have shelter and
elevation in this country to do well.

Raise from seeds and rear in pots.

CEDRUS ATLANTICA.—*Manetti*.

(The Mount Atlas Cedar.)

In Barbary, on the Mount Atlas Mountains ; at elevations 7,000ft. to
9,000ft. ; attains over 100ft. in height; timber of excellent quality and
durable.

A very ornamental tree, and deserving of cultivation. It resembles
C. Libani to a great extent when young, although much freer of growth
and of a more upright habit than that cedar.

To plant it successfully, it should have a somewhat sheltered situation,
and soil of a deep porous, marly loam. It will, however, as a rule,
grow in most soils not of a retentive nature.

Propagate from seeds. Raise the plants in pots.

CUPRESSUS SEMPERVIRENS.—*Linne*.

(The Common Erect Cypress.)

A tree indigenous to the shores of the Mediterranean, where it reaches
heights of 75 to 95ft. The timber is very durable, and is said to have
been used extensively by the ancients in the construction of the cases
made for their dead, which we now call mummies. Cases are cited
where the timber has remained in excellent condition for over 1,000
years. Undoubtedly, it is the most durable timber known.

The habit of the tree is close and upright, the same as the Lombardy
poplar. The sketch given is a fair representation of it. In long straight
avenues, or in clumps, with a good background of other kinds of trees,
it has a grand effect.

CEDRUS LIBANI.

(The Cedar of Lebanon.)

E. SPILLER LITH.

CUPRESSUS SEMPERVIRENS.

E. SPILLER, LITH.

(The Erect Cypress.)

It prefers a sandy-loam soil, with a good subsoil of a stronger character. Does well, however, on almost any site in this country. It is at the same time partial to somewhat sheltered spots, like the most of trees.

Plenty of seed can now be got from trees grown in the colony. Sow this thinly in rows or open beds in the nursery ground, and line out the seedlings 6in. apart in nursery rows for one year before planting out. The tree is very hardy and will transplant open-root with very little trouble.

CUPRESSUS SEMPERVIRENS HORIZONTALIS.—*Miller.*

(The Horizontal Cypress.)

This tree is simply a variety of the upright *C. sempervirens.* The two kinds are found growing together in their native forests, and together form one species only.

This variety is very spreading in its habit, and only grows to about 40ft. to 50ft. in height. It is a handsome tree, and well deserving of having a place in our ornamental plantations.

It is easily raised from the seed, and will grow luxuriantly in open sandy loam soil. Not partial, however, to any particular soil. It is most valuable for planting on limestone.

CUPRESSUS GOVENIANA.—*Gordon.*

(Gowen's Californian Cypress.)

A beautiful cypress, indigenous to Upper California; worthy of a place in all ornamental grounds. It is hardy, and does well in this climate.

CUPRESSUS BENTHAMI.—*Endlicher.*

(Bentham's Cypress.)

Mexico, 50 to 60ft. in height, growing at elevations 5,000 to 7,000ft. above the sea.

A beautiful tree, which delights in our climate.

Propagate from the seeds, and raise in pots.

CUPRESSUS UHDEANA.—*Gordon.*

(Uhdea's Cypress.)

SYN.—*C. Thurifera.*—Humboldt.

This is the incense-bearing Mexican cypress. A handsome tree, 50ft. high, branches spreading horizontally, sometimes pendant at tips. Indigenous to Mexico, where it is found at high elevations (7,000ft. above the sea).

A very ornamental tree, and should have a place in all pleasure-grounds and parks. It is hardy, and easily propagated from the seed.

Plant in good deep sandy-loam soil.

The tree grows excellently well about Adelaide.

G

CUPRESSUS MACROCARPA.—*Hartweg.*

(The Large-coned Cypress.)

SYN.—*C. Lambertiana.*—Gordon.

Upper California on the heights at Monterey. A large cypress of rapid growth, 100ft. in height, spreading branches, foliage a fine bright pea-green color.

Suitable for planting on comparatively dry sites, where the soil is of a sandy character and at the same time deep and porous.

The tree is hardy. Propagated from seeds. It can also be raised from cuttings.

CUPRESSUS TORULOSA. -*Don.*

(The Twisted or Bhotan Cypress.)

The Himalayan Mountains in India. A fine pyramidal tree with numerous short, slender, horizontal or sometimes deflected branches to near the ground, and drooping branchlets. Found at elevations of from 4,000ft. to 8,000ft. above the sea. (Gordon.)

This is a large tree, often reaching a height of 150ft., and from 5ft. to 6ft. in diameter. The timber is of a yellowish-red color, exceedingly fragrant, close grained, tough, long fibred, and very hard. The tree is held sacred in some parts of India, and the wood is burnt in sacred rites as incense. (Gordon.)

Not partial to any particular kind of soil.

Grows luxuriantly in our climate. Easily propagated from seed.

The following varieties are also worthy of cultivation in our pleasure grounds :—

CUPRESSUS TORULOSA VIRIDIS.—*Hort.*

A slender variety with glossy foliage.

CUPRESSUS TORULOSA MAJESTICA.—*Hort.*

More robust, larger and hardier than the species.

CUPRESSUS LAWSONIANA.—*Murray.*

(The Lawsons' Cypress.)

Indigenous to Northern California, where it grows upwards of 200ft. in height and 3-4ft. in diameter.

One of our best cypresses for ornamental planting. A magnificent tree when seen in its native forests. I give a representation of a young tree on the other side, for which I am indebted to the catalogue of the Messrs. Lawson, nurserymen, Edinburgh.

The timber is of good quality, free of knots, easily worked, and is now used for all building and railway purposes.

It may be propagated from cuttings struck in sand under glass frames, or from seeds which can now be had from the seedsmen. Sow in a box, and pot plants at the proper season.

The tree, however, requires a sheltered situation in this country. It will grow on soils ranging from a light sandy loam to a heavy clay loam.

CUPRESSUS LAWSONIANA.

(Lawson's Cypress.)

EUCALYPTUS CORYNOCALYX.

E SPILLER, LITH.

EUCALYPTUS GLOBULUS.—*La Billardiere.*

(Tasmanian Bluegum.)

Tasmania and Victoria. A very valuable tree indeed. Said to reach heights of from 250ft. to 400ft., and from 30ft. to 100ft. in circumference. Its principal habitat in Tasmania is on the south-eastern side of the island; and in Victoria, chiefly in the southern and eastern portions of the colony.—(Mueller.)

The timber is rather pale, hard, strong, and durable; its transverse strength is about equal to English oak. In durability, it occupies a medium position among that of its congeners, being more lasting than stringybark, but less durable than redgum, ironbark, and box, especially when in contact with soil or water.—(Mueller's " *Eucalyptographia.*")

The timber is used for joists, beams, rafters, studs, scantlings, ship-building, railways, carriages, agricultural implements, telegraph-poles. and for all general outdoor works. It is the most valuable tree in Tasmania.

The extraordinary properties possessed by this tree in drying up swamps and counteracting miasmatic influences are well-known all the world over. It is now being largely cultivated in different portions of the globe for these particular purposes.

It is a rapid grower, attaining heights of from 20ft. to 40ft. in a few years. Will attain to fine dimensions of timber even in poor soil, and it seems to grow in any kind of soil. It, however, delights in deep, loamy soils in somewhat sheltered situations.

This and all the *eucalypti* to follow are propagated from seeds, which can be got at any respectable seedsman's.

EUCALYPTUS CORYNOCALYX.—*Mueller.*

(Sugar Gum.)

South Australia. A large tree, reaching heights of from 80ft. to 130ft., and 3ft. to 6ft. in diameter.

The timber is hard, heavy, and durable; it is used for railway sleepers, piles, bridge-beams, scantling, &c.

A very beautiful tree. Foliage dark green and dense. Highly recommended for ornamental plantations.

This is one of the best of the *eucalypti* for planting on the plains. It will do well in very dry sites and on the tops of hills. Prefers our red, chocolate, irony soils. A rapid grower.

Does not transplant open-root well. Grow in pots or bamboos. Seed-sowing in the plantation will also be successful.

EUCALYPTUS ROSTRATA.—*Schlecht.*

(Red Gum.)

Indigenous to South Australia and Victoria. Grows to large dimensions of timber, and is found chiefly in low-lying districts where the soil is deep and where there is a plentiful supply of moisture. Heights of from 80ft. to 120ft., and 3ft. to 8ft. in diameter.

The timber is well known as being of the most valuable kind, and suitable for all underground and water works.

This tree is easily cultivated. Transplants open-root very readily. Sow seed thinly in rows in nursery ground, and transplant into plantation early in July. Thousands of seedlings can always be obtained in the natural forests of the country.

EUCALYPTUS CAROPHYLLA.—*R. Brown.*

(The Redgum of Western Australia.)

Native of Western Australia, where it grows to heights of from 100ft. to 150ft. Stems occasionally 10ft. in diameter. (Mueller.)

The tree is said to be of quicker growth than *E. Marginata*, and the timber, although not available for underground work, is used in the construction of naves, harrows, ploughs, shafts, spokes, rafters, handles, frames, rails, and other operations. (Mueller.)

This is one of the best gums for ornamental planting. The foliage is denser and more horizontal than that of any other species we know of. About Adelaide the tree does remarkably well. Well known from its large seed pods which are a very ornamental feature of the tree.

Easily reared from the seed.

EUCALYPTUS CORNUTA.—*La Billardiere.*

(The Yate Tree.)

Western Australia. A large tree with elastic and very hard wood, suitable for the manufacture of agricultural implements, boat ribs, and wheels of wagons. For cart shafts, it is almost equal to the wood of the English ash. (Mueller.)

Grows well in our climate. A rapid grower, and suitable for planting on the plains.

Delights in deep strong soils. Easily propagated from the seed.

EUCALYPTUS DIVERSICOLOR.—*Mueller.*

(The Karri Gum.)

Western Australia. One of the largest members of the *Eucalypti* family. Observed by Baron F. von Mueller about 400ft. in height. That untiring and deeply-learned botanist writes of it thus :—"Widths of timber of as much as 12ft. can be obtained from *E. diversicolor*. The wood is light-colored, bends freely, is of straight grain and tough, not so easily wrought as *E. Marginata*, and is used for shafts, spokes, felloes, rails, planks, and railway sleepers."

The tree is a rapid grower, makes a very ornamental tree in its young state, and it thrives remarkably well in this colony. I find it does best on good strong loamy soils, with a subsoil of marley clay.

Easily grown from seed. Raise in pots or bamboo tubes.

EUCALYPTUS SIDEROPHLOIA.—*Bentham.*
(The Red Ironbark.)

Queensland and New South Wales. The large-leaved "Sydney iron-bark tree," reaching a height of 150ft., with a diameter of 4ft. (Mueller's *Eucalyptographia.*)

A most valuable timber tree. The wood is hard, heavy, durable, and largely used for railway and other public works.

The tree is easily propagated from the seed. The seedlings are hardy, and transplant readily.

Succeeds well in this colony. Prefers our red chocolate soil to any other. Will grow on even somewhat dry sites.

EUCALYPTUS GOMPHOCEPHALA.—*Candolle.*
(The Tooart Gum.)

Western Australia; along the coast-line from Moore River to Geographe Bay.—(Mueller).

A valuable tree, producing a hard, close-grained, and strong timber. Reaches a height of 120ft., with proportionate girth of stem.

This tree, according to Mueller, grows only in "calcareous sandstone, formed by the wind-drifts of sea-sand." It is, therefore, a valuable tree for growing upon our *limestone* and *brackish* soils. I have already tried it with success upon sites of this character.

EUCALYPTUS PILULARIS.—*Sm.*
(The Blackbutt Gum.)

Indigenous to Victoria, Queensland, and New South Wales. A large tree, reaching 300ft. in height and 45ft. in circumference.—(Mueller's *Eucalyptographia*).

The tree is of rapid growth, timber of excellent quality, and is in use for general purposes.

Although the tree is sometimes found in high-lying districts, its chief habitat is on the flats and rich places in the valleys. It, therefore, delights in good loamy soils.

EUCALYPTUS MARGINATA. —*Smith.*
(The Jarrah Gum.)

Western Australia. 100ft. to 200ft. in height, growing in vast forests somewhat inland from the coast-line.

The most valuable of all the *Eucalypti* family as regards timber. The wood is said to be almost indestructible, and is therefore now largely used as railway sleepers, piles for bridges and jetties, and in ship-building. Resists the attacks of the white ants and the *teredo navalis* under the generality of circumstances. The wood, according to Baron von Mueller, is very strong, close-grained, slightly oily, resinous, works well, takes a fine finish, and weighs, when seasoned, about 64lbs. to the cubic foot.

Grows in poor red sandy soil, upon ironstone ridges.

I fear this will never become a tree for general planting in this part of the Australian continent. It does not seem to take kindly to our climate. There are, however, many places in the ranges where it could be grown here, but it is not suitable for planting on our plains.

EUCALYPTUS HEMIPHLOIA.—*Mueller.*
(Box Gum.)

South Australia. A fine timber tree; several varieties in the colony; excellent timber, hard, heavy, and durable; grows 60ft. to 80ft. in height. A hardy tree, and suitable for planting in exposed and poor situations.

EUCALYPTUS LEUCOXYLON.—*Mueller.*
(S. A. Bluegum.)

South Australia and Victoria. From 80ft. to 100ft. in height.; most valuable timber, heavy, hard, and durable. Used for sleepers, naves, felloes, spokes, joists, beams, telegraph poles, piles, &c.
Highly recommended for planting upon limestone country.

EUCALYPTUS ODORATA.—*Behr.*
(Peppermint Gum)

South Australia. 60ft. to 70ft. in height; heavy, tough, and durable timber. Used for same purposes as *E. Leucoxylon.*
Will grow on limestone soils.

EUCALYPTUS GIGANTEA.—*Hooker.*
(The Stringybark of Tasmania.)

One of the largest trees in Tasmania; attains a height of 200ft. to 350ft. This is the tree which yields the famous "Tasmanian palings," with which everyone is now so familiar.
I find it to grow healthily and rapidly in good, deep, red chocolate soils in sheltered situations.

EUCALYPTUS OBLIQUA.—*L'Herit.*
(S. A. Stringybark.)

Our best gum for splitting, and general economic purposes; over 100ft. in height. Timber used for fencing, scantlings, boards, shingles, palings, rafters, scaffolding poles, and machinery.
Prefers a good elevation, and soil of a rough, sandy, ironstone nature.

FICUS MACROPHYLLA.—*Desf.*
(Moreton Bay Fig Tree.)

This is the large-leaved specia of this family with which we are all so familiar about Adelaide. It is a native of Queensland, where it attains heights ranging from 50ft. to 100ft., and 2ft. to 3ft. in diameter. Evergreen; leaves cordate and oblong, and of a bright dark-shining green color.

FRAXINUS EXCELSIOR.

(The English Ash.)

E SPILLER, LITH

This is one of our most valuable shade trees. It will grow on almost any kind of soil, and is especially valuable for planting on calcareous soils. It is subject to be injured by frosts in its young stage, and should therefore be protected for a few months each winter, where frosts are troublesome, until it reaches 5ft. or 6ft. in height.

The timber is of no particular value.

Can be grown easily from seeds sown in boxes, and the young plants put in good-sized pots.

FRAXINUS EXCELSIOR.—*Linn.*
(The Common English Ash.)

All parts of Europe. 90ft. to 100ft. in height and 3ft. to 4ft. in diameter.

Delights in low-lying and sheltered situations, with plenty of moisture, though free from anything like stagnant water. Will grow on sidelings where there is a deep retentive subsoil.

The timber is of the most valuable description, and for toughness and elasticity is unsurpassed by any other European tree. It is largely used by the carpenter, wheelwright, basketmaker, coachmaker, sievewright, and for the construction of tool handles, crates, hoops, &c.

The tree is a rapid grower. It suits itself to the climate of this country. Now largely planted in the forest reserves.

Can be raised from seeds or cuttings sown and laid in in August.

FRAXINUS AMERICANA.—*Linn.*
(The American White Ash.)

North America. A very valuable tree, growing luxuriantly on deep vegetable soils in swamps and on the banks of the rivers. Attains heights of 100ft. to 150ft. and diameters 2ft. to 3½ft.

Celebrated for the strength and durability of its timber, which is now largely used in the construction of agricultural implements, wagons, carriages, axe handles, &c. Possesses great lateral strength.

A very ornamental tree when allowed room to spread out its branches. The tree is rather given to make side-shoots, which should be curtailed in plantations formed for timber growing, by thick planting.

Succeeds well in this country when planted in good deep marly or loamy soil, so long as there is plenty of moisture percolating through it. It also requires shelter from the hot winds. In the Wirrabara Forest Reserve we have it 6ft. to 9ft. in height at eighteen months old.

Grown from seeds or cuttings, both of which should be put out in the open nursery ground in August month.

FRENELA ROBUSTA.—*Cunn.*
(The Native Pine.)

A highly ornamental tree, indigenous to our colony. Generally found in poor, sandy soils; 40ft. to 50ft. in height.

Suitable for planting on calcareous soils. Easily reared by simply sowing the seed on nice clean soil in the plantation.

GREVILLEA ROBUSTA.—*A. Cunn.*
(The Silky Oak.)

Queensland. A large tree 80ft. to 100ft. in height, and 2½ft. to 3½ft. in diameter. Evergreen, strong robust looking tree ; pyramidical in shape, with stout stem.

The timber is of good quality, and is extensively used for staves for tallow casks, and is in much repute for cabinet work. (R. Hill.)

Adapts itself to our climate. Many fine specimens are now about Adelaide.

Propagate from seed, of which abundance can now be got from trees grown in the colony. Sow in boxes, and transplant seedlings into pots. Protect from frost, and plant out in July-August.

LAGUNARIA PATERSONI.—*Don.*

On the River Don, Queensland, 40ft. to 60ft. in height, and 18in. to 30in. in diameter. The timber is white, close-grained, and easily worked. (Hill.)

Adapts itself to our climate, and seems to grow well here on almost any soil and in any situation.

Readily raised from the seed, which can now be got in abundance from the trees about Adelaide.

MELIA AZEDARACH.—*Linne.*
(The Persian Lilac, or Bead Tree.)

India and Syria. A well-known deciduous tree, which luxuriates in our climate. Here called " white cedar." One of our best trees for avenues. (See sketch.) Very handsome, with sweet-scented flowers.

Seeds plentiful about Adelaide. Sow in rows in open nursery ground.

PINUS CANARIENSIS.—*Smith.*
(The Canary Island Pine.)

Canary Islands. A large tree 70ft. to 80ft. in height, ascending on the mountains and Peak of Teneriffe from 5,000ft. to 7,200ft. of elevation. There are extensive forests of it on the Grand Canary Islands, at elevations, chiefly, of about 4,000ft. to 6,000ft. (Gordon.)

The leaves are long, slender, bright green, somewhat pendulous, cones long and broad, and with a hard shining surface. The seeds are large, with wings attached.

The timber is very resinous, durable, and said to be free from attacks of insects.

Succeeds well in a variety of soils. It is partial, however, to those of a sharp sandy loam nature, with plenty of depth. Grows well on high-lying and exposed sites.

The tree is somewhat shy of transplanting. It is deficient in fibrous roots, and must, therefore, at all times be grown in pots for safe transplanting ; grows quickly, and is a very handsome and ornamental tree.

It does excellently well in our climate.

MELIA   AZEDARACH.

(White Cedar.)

E. SPILLER, LITH.

PINUS SABINIANA.—*Douglas.*
(Sabine's Pine.)

Indigenous to California. Found at high elevations chiefly, and generally intermixed with other kinds of trees. Foliage long and graceful, shape pyramidical, heights ranging from 90ft. to 150ft., and diameters 2ft. to 5ft.

The timber is somewhat soft and not very durable.

The tree grows rapidly in this country, and is worthy of cultivation. It does well in somewhat dry sites where the soil is light, but it prefers good loamy soils and sheltered spots.

Produces large cones. The seeds are edible.

PINUS COULTERI.—*Don.*
(The Large-coned Pine.)
Syn. P. Macrocarpa (Lindley).

California, at elevations 3,000ft. to 4,000ft. A free-growing and beautifully-shaped pine, attaining from 90ft. to 100ft. in height and 3ft. to 4ft. in diameter. A fine tree for ornamental planting. The timber is of an average quality.

It requires a good sheltered site with a soil of a deep light loamy nature, and not cold or retentive in the subsoil.

There are some good specimens to be seen about Adelaide.

PINUS JEFFREYII.—*Balfour.*
(Jeffrey's Pine.)

Northern California. A rapid grower; handsome tree, 150ft. in height, and 4ft. in diameter. Prefers sandy soils in its native country. It, however, does well here in soils ranging from a sandy to a clayey loam. Requires a sheltered situation in this country.

The timber is said to be of good average quality. There is, however, not much reliable information on the subject.

It requires some attention in raising here.

PINUS INSIGNIS.—*Douglas.*
(The Remarkable Pine.)

California, where it grows 80ft. to 120ft. in height, and over 3ft. in diameter. Tall, graceful, and regular in outline, with nicely-feathered branches from the ground upwards.

This is one of the few introductions of pines to the colony which have succeeded to the best of expectations in our climate. It is a very rapid grower, and seems to adapt itself to all conditions of soil and locality. Its most favorable situation, however, is that somewhat low-lying, well sheltered, on a soil of a deep, light, marly loam, with a good retentive subsoil. It ought to be extensively cultivated in this country.

The timber is of good quality and is in general use in California.

I have found the tree to transplant open-root very readily here.

Easily raised from seeds. Sow in boxes and transplant into lines or pots, as the case may be.

PINUS PINEA.—*Linne.*

(Stone Pine.)

South of Europe, North Africa, and Asia, bordering on the Mediterranean Sea, in which countries it presents a marked feature in the landscape.

From 50ft. to 60ft. in height.   In sketch adjoining I show its general character, although in many cases it will have a more bushy appearance than is presented there.

The timber is light, of a whitish color, and very resinous.   Used in house-building and furniture making.

The tree delights in situations of a deep light and stony character, grows well on limestone ridges, for which habit it is of great value here.

It succeeds admirably in the colony.   The seeds, which are large and edible, can now be had in any quantity about town, and may be got cheap from the seedsmen.

Sow and rear the same as the other pines.

PINUS RADIATA.—*Don.*

(The Radiated Cone Pine.)

On the coast of Upper California. Chiefly solitary, in masses by itself, 80ft. to 100ft. in height, and 3ft. in diameter, according to soil and situation.

Tall, fine upright growth, well clothed with branches, and a very rapid grower.

Some writers confound this species with *P. insignis*, to which in many ways it has a strong resemblance.   The general appearance of both trees is equal, but the leaves are more slender and shorter, and the cones are three times longer in *P. radiata* than in the other.

An excellent pine for planting on the sea-coast, even within the influence of the salt water.

Excellent timber, which is used for boat-building in California.

Propagate from seeds sown in boxes, and afterwards line out or pot, as already directed.

PINUS LONGIFOLIA.—*Roxburgh.*

(The " Cheer" or Long-leaved Pine.)

India, along the hot valleys of the Sikkim, or the stony hills of the Punjaub, and on the foot-hills of the Himalaya mountains.   Found at elevations ranging from 1,000ft. to 7,000ft. above the sea.

A tree 60ft. to 100ft. in height, hardy, very ornamental; seeds large and edible. Wood of excellent quality, and used for house-building.

The tree does well in our climate.   It is hardy and easily raised from the seed.   Partial to sheltered situations and good loamy soils.

PINUS HALEPENSIS.—*Ait.*

(The Aleppo Pine.)

Indigenous chiefly to the countries lying along the coast of the Mediterranean Sea.   Grows from 50ft. to 90ft. in height, with good diameters ranging from 2ft. to 3½ft.

PINUS   PINEA.

(Stone Pine.)

E SPILLER LITH

The timber is of excellent quality; it is white, soft, and possesses a very fine grain. Used for many purposes connected with ship-building and house-building. According to Baron Mueller, the tree yields a Venetian turpentine as well as a valuable tar.

This tree has been planted with great success in South Australia. It ranks next to *P. insignis* as our most successful introduction of exotic trees. On all sites not positively dry or barren it will make a fair attempt to grow. It, however, delights in soils of a sandy nature on top, with a good marly clay in the subsoil. A rapid grower, and should be largely planted.

Seeds can be readily procured from our seedsmen. Sow as usual. Plant out into the plantation in June or July.

PINUS PINASTER.—*Ait.*

(The Cluster Pine)
Syn P. Maritima.—Lamarck.

A very valuable pine, indigenous to the south of Europe, northern shores of Africa, and the west of Asia. Derives its name from the cones, which are from 6in. to 8in. in length, being in clusters or groups of from three to eight together, which point out, or radiate from a centre like the spokes of a wheel.

If allowed room to grow, it forms a very fine, spreading, and bold, massive-looking tree, though at all times somewhat rugged. From 70ft. to 80ft. in height.

Although the timber is not of the very best description, it is extensively used in the south of Europe for such purposes as house-building, boxes, &c.

This tree will not grow well at a high elevation. It delights in low-lying places near the sea; indeed, unless it is within the influence of the seabreeze it is not likely to succeed. The nearer to the sea the better will the result be. Withstands the withering effects of the sea blasts to perfection. In this respect, therefore, it is one of our most valuable trees for seaside planting.

The tree has a strong tap root, which soon penetrates deeply into the soil. From this fact, if it be planted on the coast, it soon establishes itself beyond the influence of the dry weather. Large tracts of barren shifting sands in France and the Cape of Good Hope have been permanently improved and put under a good crop of timber of this tree by simply sowing the seed broadcast at the proper season.

Its favorite soil is a deep sandy loam. It will not grow on limestone country.

Propagate from seeds, which can now be procured from trees grown in the colony.

PLATANUS ACERIFOLIA.—*Willd.*

(The Maple-leaved Plane.)

South of Europe. 70ft to 90ft. in height; a rapid grower; deciduous, and a very ornamental tree.

The timber is soft, and not of any commercial value. It is, however, used in cabinet work.

This is, perhaps, the best of the plane-trees for growing in the colony. It is hardy, grows freely, and adapts itself to our climate. An excellent tree for street and avenue planting. It is easily reared, safely transplanted, and does well in most soils free of limestone. As instances of its growth and beauty, I would refer to the avenue of it along King William Road, and that in the Botanic Park.

Propagate from cuttings, seeds, or layers; the former is, perhaps, the most profitable way in this climate. Cuttings can now be procured in abundance about Adelaide.

PLATANUS OCCIDENTALIS.—*Linne.*
(American Plane Tree.)

North America generally. A fine ornamental tree, 70ft. to 80ft. in height when full grown; deciduous; of comparatively rapid growth; habit somewhat more upright than the other plane trees. It may easily be distinguished from its congener—*Platanus Orientalis*—by its red petioles and large and smooth fruit.

Timber soft, short-grained, and easily broken; sometimes used by the cabinetmakers.

Must have a deep porous soil, with plenty of moisture; to do well in this climate it must have choice sites.

Propagate from seeds or cuttings: the latter way preferable here.

PLATANUS ORIENTALIS.—*Linne.*
(The Oriental Plane Tree.)

The Levant, Asia Minor, and Persia. Some 80ft. in height. A noble tree, with a fine ornamental appearance. Well adapted for cultivation in towns and parks. The timber is used by cabinetmakers and carpenters. Delights in deep, light, moist soils, and in sheltered situations.

Do not attempt to grow it in exposed places here. In hollows, ravines, glens, and other shaded places, however, it will do well, especially if planted amongst other trees.

Propagate from cuttings, layers, or seeds. I prefer the former method in this country. Line out in rows July or August.

POPULUS ALBA.—*Linne.*
(White Poplar.)

One of the most valuable of our European poplars. Deciduous; foliage of a blackish-green above and silvery downy-white beneath. It has several varieties which differ chiefly in the character of the foliage and hardiness of constitution.

The timber is soft, light, white, and stringy, not subject to swelling or shrinking, and is valuable in the manufacture of toys, trays, flooring, shoe-soles, and wooden plates.

Succeeds well in this climate. There are some excellent specimens at Highercombe, Mount Gambier, and the Botanic Gardens.

In Europe this tree is not easily propagated by cuttings. Here, however, I find it not at all difficult to raise plants of the kind in this way. The tree throws off many suckers, which can always be safely utilised. A piece of a root will also produce a good plant.

POPULUS MONILIFERA.—*Ait.*

(Black Italian Poplar.)

Sometimes called the " Necklace-bearing poplar," from the peculiar shape of the catkins upon the female tree having a resemblance to that article of ladies' attire. Native of North America, where it attains heights of from 80ft. to 100ft. The habit is more upright than the common black poplar, although the branches are more spreading and less clinging to the stem of the tree than is the case in the latter one.

The tree is a very rapid grower. Even in the cold climate of Scotland, it occasionally reaches a height of 70ft. in sixteen years. The rate of growth is even much greater than that in this country, where it succeeds reasonably well.

The timber is of good quality, and in Italy is largely used for such purposes as packing-boxes, planking for grape carts, and turner's work.

Can be grown from either the seed or cuttings—the latter way will do best here. Line these out in the nursery in the usual way.

POPULUS FASTIGIATA.—*Desf.*

(Upright or Lombardy Poplar.)

Indigenous to middle and south of Europe, particularly to Lombardy, also to some portions of Asia Minor. Deciduous tree, tall upright habit, a rapid grower, hardy constitution, with the lateral branches closely gathered to the stem.

The timber is light, not very durable, and not generally in use for any particular commercial purpose. For the general outside work of a farm, however, this tree, from its quick growth, will produce much that will be of service. For posts, rails, sheep hurdles, &c., it will be found of great advantage.

The growth of the tree is something really wonderful, and is only equalled by that of the *Eucalyptus globulus* (the Tasmanian Bluegum). In this country especially, it grows very rapidly, and has become a very desirable addition to our arborous flora.

As a rule the tree grows well in any soil so long as there is moisture in the subsoil. To see it, however, in its most flourishing condition, it should be planted in a deep loamy soil, with plenty of running water within its reach. Grows from 120ft. to 170ft. in height in forty to fifty years.

As an ornamental tree it is of great value to mix with trees of a more branchy and horizontal character. Its tall upright form has a very fine effect when seen towering above masses of other kinds of trees.

From its close compact shape, and the fact of its being little injured by smoke, the tree is a good one for planting in towns and cities. Makes an imposing avenue tree. It can be grown very closely together; and from this fact I have recommended it as a good shelter-hedge. (See Figs. 50, 51, 52, and 53.)

Grows well in this colony, where fine large specimens may now be seen of it in different parts.

Propagate by cuttings put out in nursery lines July or August.

POPULUS CANESCENS.—*Smith.*
(The Grey Poplar.)

The common English white poplar. 50ft. to 80ft. in height; spreading; timber valuable for rollers, packing cases, turners' work, toys, flooring boards, and other purposes requiring soft wood.

Plant in loamy soils with plenty of moisture. It will, however, also grow well in other kinds of soils.

Propagate by cuttings, layers, and suckers.

POPULUS NIGRA.—*Linne.*
(The Common Black Poplar.)

Europe. 70ft. to 90ft. in height, and 3ft. in diameter, growing rapidly, and forming an ornamental tree. The wood is yellow, soft, and splits easily. It is used by cartwrights, turners, and cabinetmakers.

Plant in strong loamy soil, moist in the subsoil, though not cold nor retentive.

Can be readily propagated by cuttings.

POPULUS ANGULATA.—*Ait.*
(The Angle-Branched or Carolina Poplar.)

America. Seventy to 80ft. high. A very ornamental tree. The wood is not of much value.

Propagated by layers and cuttings.

POPULUS MACROPHYLLA.
(The Ontario Poplar.)

Indigenous to North America, where it attains a height of over 90ft. Very rapid in growth; has large heart-shaped leaves, and gummy buds, with an agreeable balsamic odour.

Grows best on banks of streams, and other dampish spots. It is very easily propagated from cuttings.

QUERCUS PEDUNCULATA.—*Wield.*
(The Common English Oak.)

All over Europe and northern parts of Asia and Africa. Deciduous. 80-100 ft. in height. Leaves with short petioles, and the acorns with long foot-stalks. A massive tree, large trunk, spreading and gnarled limbs when in old age; ornamental in all its features (see sketch), and a long liver.

QUERCUS PEDUNCULATA.

(English Oak.)

E. SPILLER, LITH.

The tree is a slow grower, as a rule, in its indigenous forests, and even in our fine climate its growth is, comparatively speaking, slow, although much more rapid than it is at home.

To grow to perfection, it requires a strong, heavy, clayey soil, with plenty of moisture, combined with good natural drainage. The tree will, however, grow well in most soils, so long as the roots have plenty of water in the summer time, and the situation is sheltered. It is not suitable for planting on the exposed plains of the colony, but in our higher-lying and cooler regions it may be cultivated with good chance of success.

One of the most valuable timber-trees in Europe. The quality of the timber is too well known to require any description here.

There are some excellent specimens of the tree now in the colony.

The acorns, of which hundreds of bushels can now be procured in the colony, should be sown in rows as soon as possible after collection (the acorns 3in. to 4in. from one another, and the rows 15in. apart). The young plants should be transplanted into the nursery lines for a year before they are put out into the plantations.

QUERCUS SESSILIFLORA.—*Sal.*

(The British Sessile-flowered Oak.)

Indigenous to the same countries as *Q. Pedunculata*. General appearance much the same as the other. In this specia, however, the petioles of the leaves are long, while the fruit, or acorns, are entirely without stalks.

More of an upright growth than *Q. Pedunculata;* timber somewhat heavier and more generally serviceable; grows on similar soils, though, if anything, it will succeed on a greater variety of sites than the other.

Propagation, same as *Q. Pedunculata*. Seeds easily procured from trees in the Mount Lofty hills, where it grows with vigor.

QUERCUS CERRIS.—*Linn.*

(Turkey Oak.)

Deciduous, 60ft. to 100ft. in height; native of southern Europe and parts of Asia. Form of tree—somewhat spreading and inclined to droop. Of a much quicker growth than the English oaks just described.

The timber is said to be inferior in quality to that of its English congeners, although at the same time it is of considerable value, and available for wheelwrights, coachmakers, turners, and coopers. (Mueller.) It is, however, finer in the grain and takes on a better polish.

The tree requires comparatively sheltered situations, and soils of a deep character to grow to perfection. It succeeds fairly well in the cooler regions of the colony. Not available for open exposed planting here.

Cultivate from acorns sown and managed in the nursery the same as those of the other oaks.

ROBINIA PSEUDO-ACACIA.—*Linn.*
(Common or False Acacia.)

Deciduous, 40ft. to 50ft. in height; indigenous to North America, where it is known as the "Locust tree." A rapid grower with very ornamental foliage. The timber is valuable, being close-grained, hard, and beautifully veined. It is useful for the purposes of the wheelwright, shipwright, and cabinetmaker; very durable—instances being known where it has remained good in the ground for over 80 years. When dry the timber weighs over 50lbs. per cubic foot. Its tensile strength is also of a very high standard.

As an ornamental tree it is also to be recommended. The flowers are white and possess a sweet odour.

The tree is now well-known in the colony, where it is called the *White Acacia*.

It luxuriates in light deep sandy soils, but will grow in this country in almost any situation. The tree throws off numerous suckers which make excellent plants for transplanting.

Easily propagated from the seed, which can now be readily obtained from trees grown in the colony.

SALIX BABYLONICA—*Tournefort.*
(The Weeping Willow.)

Asia, on the banks of the Euphrates, near Babylon, whence its name; and also of China and other parts of Asia; and of Egypt and other parts of the north of Africa. Height 39ft. to 50ft.—(Loudon.)

A well-known tree, highly ornamental (see sketch opposite), affording excellent shade, and a rapid grower in our climate.

The tree prefers moist situations, with deep loamy soils. It will, however, also grow exceedingly well in most situations which are not absolutely dry.

Easily propagated from cuttings.

SCHINUS MOLLE.—*Linn.*
(The Pepper Tree.)

Evergreen. A native of Peru, where it grows 15ft. to 20ft. in height. It is well-known in the colony, and is largely planted about Adelaide as an ornamental tree-shrub.

For intermixing with other trees in ornamental grounds, it is highly serviceable. The foliage is graceful and airy looking, especially in its young stage. It is of rapid growth, and will grow well upon most kinds of soil, including those of a calcareous nature.

Propagate from the seed, which can be procured at the seedsmen. Sow in boxes, and transplant into pots.

STERCULIA ACERIFOLIA.—*A. Cunn.*
(The Flame Tree.)

An evergreen tree, indigenous to Queensland. Its bright-red flowers have a grand appearance. Propagate from the seed. Sow in boxes and put out in pots afterwards.

SALIX BABYLONICA.

(The Weeping Willow.)

E SPILLER LITH

STERCULIA HETEROPHYLLA.—*Beauv.*

Perhaps the best of our Sterculias. Evergreen ; grandly magnificent in its outlines for ornamental planting. Highly suitable for lines of trees where uniformity of size and shape are required, such as in avenues.

Plant in sandy-loam soils. Propagate from seed, which can be procured in abundance from the trees now growing about Adelaide.

TAMARIX GALLICA.—*Linn.*
(Tamarisk Tree.)

A small feathery-looking shrub, of some 12ft. to 15ft. in. height, indigenous to South Europe, Asia, and Africa. It is admirably adapted for planting on the sea-coast as a hedge and shelter plant. In most situations it is recommended as a hedge plant.

A fast grower, and easily propagated by cuttings put in in July or August.

Baron Mueller says of it—" It will grow alike in water and the driest soil, also in salty ground, and is one of the most grateful and tractable plants in culture."

It is now quite common about Adelaide, and cuttings can be obtained without much trouble or expense.

ULMUS CAMPESTRIS.—*Linn.*
(English Elm.)

Europe and Asia. Deciduous ; luxuriates in deep, rich, dry soils of a loose and free nature, in which it will attain to large dimensions of timber. Reaches heights 80ft. to 100ft , and 4ft. to 5ft. in diameter.

Produces one of our most valuable timbers ; this is of great durability, very elastic and tough, and is much used in the construction of naves, spokes, blocks, furniture, keels, and other works where strength in a small compass is looked for.

The tree, when planted in a congenial spot, is a free grower. The contour of the tree is massive and graceful looking, and the foliage is a dark green.

Grows well in this country. On the plains it is of somewhat slow growth, but once let it get well established and surrounded by other kinds of trees, and it will go ahead even upon these.

Propagation is done by seeds (which are now common in the colony), and also by cuttings, and layers.

ULMUS MONTANA.—*Smith.*
(The Scots or Wych Elm.)

Britain and Continent of Europe. From 80ft. to 100ft. in height. Deciduous ; large deeply serrated leaves. The tree has a strong spreading habit, with a large head, and the branches at maturity have a drooping tendency at the ends, which gives the tree a fine ornamental effect. As an ornamental tree this is highly recommended. A rapid

H

In the older plantations, look over the young trees and shorten back any inferior growths which seem to be interfering with the proper ascendancy of the leaders; shorten lateral branches, and otherwise liberate thriving young trees.

Hedges which are somewhat bare in the bottom, may very judiciously be lopped at this time in order to throw the growth of the plants into making fresh shoots among the bottom branches. Keep all hedges clean and the soil stirred about the roots of the plants.

In the nursery, attend to keeping down all weeds, and hoe the soil round all young trees lined out in rows. Rub off and prune all unnecessary shoots on deciduous trees. Keep the shades on seedling plants and water regularly at night. Take shades off at night and put on again next morning, if the sun comes out hot. Water potted plants every night.

FEBRUARY.

Go on with pruning work in the plantations. Any large limbs which it is desirable to have removed from trees should be lopped this month; but do work of this kind sparingly, and, if possible, by shortening only. Pile the prunings and keep them in open spaces as much as possible away from the trees, or remove them altogether.

Continue care and attention to the young trees in the plantations, and water them if possible. Be sure to loosen the soil round the stems next day after watering. Freshen up all mulching.

Look out for bush fires and continue precautions against these.

Continue fallowing ground for planting.

The first sowing of *Eucalypti* seed may be sown about the end of this month. Other nursery operations to be continued as directed in last month's calendar.

Cut hedges and dig round the roots of the plants.

This and the next three months are suitable for felling timber, in order that good durable wood may be obtained.

MARCH.

Prepare the large holes for plants, where ploughing and other preparations are not considered necessary. In doing this, keep the subsoil on one side, and the top soil by itself on another side. These holes should now remain open until planting time, in order that the soil may get thoroughly pulverised and in a nice mellow condition for the roots of the young plants to be put into it.

This is often another dry and very trying month for the young plants in the plantations. Every care should therefore be taken of them in the manner elsewhere described.

This is a good time for general pruning and thinning in the plantations, and this operation ought to be pushed forward about this season of the year.

In order to secure there being plenty of plants of the *Eucalypti* species for the coming season's planting, it is as well to put in another sowing of the seeds of such kinds of trees—that is, where the plants are raised in boxes or bamboos.

Make final pruning and trimming up of the deciduous plants in the nursery, which are intended to be planted out during the approaching season.

Further all operations connected with the preparation of the ground for the approaching planting.

Keep hardening off all gums and pines in the manner directed.

APRIL.

Plants of first sowing in bamboos should be moved this month, and given less water, in order to check their growth and harden the young wood before the planting season comes on.

If the weather is of a character to admit of such work being done, have the ground intended to be planted thoroughly subsoiled with the plough, to the depth of 15in. or more, as elsewhere recommended and described in the body of this work. This remark has reference, of course, only to such land as may not have been previously treated in this manner. The performing this operation early in the season will allow of the winter's rain sinking deep down into the soil, and being stored for the use of the plants during the summer months. Let the ground remain rough, so that it may moulder down with the rains which are to follow.

Push on all pruning and thinning operations in the plantations.

Potted and bamboo plants should now receive plenty of cool air about them, and, unless the weather continues unusually warm for the season, they may do without much attention in the way of water and shade. The great point is to keep hardening them as much as possible, so that they may be able to withstand the change of situation when put out in the plantation.

Sow all pine seeds in boxes for potting out in the months of July to September, as may be found most advantageous in accordance with the prevailing weather at the time.

Sinking the holes for the reception of the young plants may be done this month, as well as during March.

MAY.

Subsoiling the proposed plantation ground should be finished not later than the end of this month.

All pruning and thinning in the plantations to be finished during this month.

Should the weather be favorable, planting may be begun this month.

JUNE.

If the weather is dull and favorable after the middle of the month, and the deciduous trees have lost their leaves, begin to plant them out from the nursery into the plantations. Let the plants be carefully raised from the lines with as much of their fibrous roots attached as possible. Only get up as many plants each morning as will keep the men busy putting in during the day. As soon as they are raised, have them conveyed to the plantation and *laid in* the ground at convenient spots along the line of planting. Be careful to see that the roots are exposed to the air for as short a time as possible. Too great care cannot be displayed in these matters.

Keep all gums in pots, bamboo tubes, or boxes, on a high dry site and well sheltered from any frosts which may occur. Give them just as much water as they can exist upon, and no more.

Dig the soil up rough for a few feet round the stems of the trees in last year's plantations. Be careful, of course, not to go too deep near the trees, so as to cut or disturb their roots.

If the weather be favorable, general planting should begin this month.

The sowing of tree seeds in the plantations where this system of rearing trees is adopted, should be done early this month.

JULY.

The planting out of pines and other hardy species of trees should be finished during this month. Scarify or plough the ground, if possible, before planting it, in order to kill the young grass and weeds which will now begin to make their appearance upon it. Any wet and boggy ground had better be left out from this planting until later on in the spring-time.

Plant hedges. Pot pines.

AUGUST.

Push on all planting. As soon as the hardier kinds of trees, referred to under the heading of last month, are all put out, proceed with the planting of the different kinds of *Eucalypti* plants. Protect these as they are put out, as directed elsewhere in this work. If possible, planting should be finished by the end of this month, but, of course, much will depend upon the character of the season as to whether the operations can be continued later or not.

Continue nursery work. Put in all cuttings, and sow seeds of deciduous and·pine trees, for open-root growing in the nursery. Transplant seedlings from beds and boxes into the nursery rows.

Hoe the soil round all the trees planted during the previous two months.

Late hedges may be planted this month.

SEPTEMBER.

Keep hoeing round all trees planted during the season. See that all the protection guards are kept in good order.

Any blanks which may have occurred in the season's planting, should be filled up as early as possible during this month.

Keep down all weeds in the plantations, and scarify between the rows of trees. The more the soil is stirred about the trees during this month, the better will the result be.

Late nursery work should be completed early this month.

OCTOBER.

Sow pine seeds for potting in January.

The weather may now be expected to be pretty warm. Keep hoeing and digging round all plants; then, if the weather seems to indicate the setting in of dry hot days with little or no rain, proceed with the mulching of such of the young plants as may require it.

Keep the scarifier going in the plantations, and plough all fire-breaks.

Plough ground intended for next season's planting operations.

Look over young plantations, and check back any branches which appear to interfere with the growth of the leaders.

NOVEMBER.

Proceed with hoeing, digging, and mulching, and keep looking to the young trees, to check lateral shoots, and encourage upward growth.

Scarify and harrow all fire-breaks, and collect and burn, or otherwise dispose of any inflammable matter which may be upon them.

Attend to young hedges and keep them clear of weeds.

See to deciduous plants in the nursery, and rub off all superfluous buds, &c. Keep nursery clean, and hoe between the rows of plants.

Prepare boxes and bamboo tubes for *Eucalypti* plants.

DECEMBER.

The weather will now be very hot and dry. Pay every attention to the young plants. Hoe round them after every shower of rain, should there be any at this time; at all events, do not let the soil get baked about them. Frequent hoeing at this time will rush the plants on wonderfully. Water the plants if possible.

Bush fires may now be looked for. If previous instructions have been properly attended to, the plantations will be quite safe from them. Scarify and harrow the fire-breaks as directed.

Scarify the ploughed ground intended for the next year's plantation, should this appear to be necessary.

See to the hedges, and look to the plants in the nursery, as directed for the previous month.

CHAPTER XXIX.

Trees Suitable for Planting on the Plains.

WITH good soil, plenty of moisture, a temperate atmosphere, and a sheltered situation, it is at all times an easy matter for good results to be obtained with ordinary care by the general planter in the higher-lying regions of our glorious country; but when he has to cope with a short water supply, a bleak open site subject to fiercely-hot and bitterly-cold winds such as are experienced on the plains of our northern areas, his work is one beset with difficulties, and often ends in bitter disappointments. These plains of ours are somewhat peculiar ones, and although possessing soils of great depth and of the richest description, they are, generally speaking, so much exposed and uninviting, that at present it is only a limited list of trees which will grow upon them with any degree of health and rapid growth. No doubt this will undergo great and important changes for the better as the country gets more densely populated and the hedges and plantations begin to exert their influence upon its atmospheric condition. At the present time, however, we have got to cope with the conditions such as they exist, and do the best we can under the circumstances.

With the view, then, of preventing disappointments by the inexperienced planting unsuitable trees, I give the following as a list of those kinds which may be expected to do well on the more exposed portions of the plains :—

Acacia Pycnantha—(Benth.) .... " Broad-leaved Wattle."

Cupressus Sempervirens—(Linne.) .... "The Common Erect Cypress."

Cupressus Sempervirens Horizontalis—(Miller) "The Horizontal Cypress."

Eucalyptus Globulus—(La Billard.) .... "The Tasmanian Bluegum."

Eucalyptus Corynocalyx—(Mueller.) .... "The Sugar Gum."

Eucalyptus Rostrata—(Sch.) .... "The Red Gum."

Eucalyptus Carophylla—(R. Brown.)........ "The Red Gum of W. A."

Eucalyptus Cornuta—(La Billard.) .... "The Yate Gum."

Eucalyptus Diversicolor—(Mueller.) .... "The Karri Gum."

Eucalyptus Siderophloia—(Bentham) ...... "The Red Ironbark."

Eucalyptus Leucoxylon—(Mueller.).......... "The S. A. Bluegum."

Eucalyptus Odorata—(Behr.) .... "The Peppermint Gum."

Ficus Macrophylla—(Derf.)............... "The Moreton Bay Fig."

Lagunaria Patersoni—(Don.) ....   *   *   *
Pinus Canariensis—(Smith.) .... "The Canary Island Pine."
Pinus Insignis—(Douglas.) .... "The Remarkable Pine."
Pinus Pinea—(Linne.) .... "The Stone Pine."
Pinus Longifolia.—(Rox.) .... "The Cheer Pine."
Pinus Halepensis.—(Ait.) .... "The Aleppo Pine."
Pinus Pinaster.—(Ait.) .... "The Cluster Pine."
Populus Fastigiata.—(Desf.) .... "The Lombardy Poplar."
Robinia Pseudo-Acacia.—(Linn.) .... "The False Acacia."
Schinus Molle.—(Linn.) .... "The Pepper Tree."
Tamarix Gallica.—(Linn.) .... "The Tamarisk Tree."

CHAPTER XXX.

Trees Suitable for Avenue Planting.

TREES may be planted as avenues under a variety of circumstances. We may have them along public roads, through parks, on approach-roads to country residences, in large gardens, and so on.

The following list embraces the best kinds of those species of trees now growing in the colony, which are suitable for the formation of avenues :—

Cupressus Sempervirens—(Linn.)	" The Common Erect Cypress."
Cupressus Sempervirens Horizontalis—(Miller.)	" The Common Horizontal Cypress"
Eucalyptus Corynocalyx—(Mueller.)	" The Sugar Gum."
Ficus Macrophylla—(Desf.)	" Moreton Bay Fig."
Fraxinus Excelsior—(Linn.).	" The English Ash."
Fraxinus Americana—(Linn.)	" The American White Ash."
Lagunaria Patersoni—(Don.)..............	* * *
Melia Azedarach—(Linn.)	" The White Cedar."
Pinus Insignis—(Douglas.)	" The Remarkable Pine."
Pinus Halepensis—(Ait.)	" The Aleppo Pine."
Platanus Acerifolia—(Willd.)	" The Maple-leaved Plane."
Populus Monilifera—(Ait.)	" The Black Italian Poplar."
Populus Fastigiata—(Desf.)	" The Upright or Lombardy Poplar."
Populus Alba—(Linn.)	" The White Poplar."
Robinia Pseudo-Acacia—(Linn.)	" The Common or False Acacia."
Sterculia Heterophylla—(Beauv.)	" The Flame Tree."
Ulmus Campestris—(Linn.)	" The English Elm."
Ulmus Montana—(Smith.)	" The Scotch Elm."
Ulmus Suberosa—(Ehrh.)..............	" The Cork Elm."

CHAPTER XXXI.

~~~❧❀❧~~~

Trees Suitable for Planting on Saline Soils.

SOILS impregnated with saline matter, of which we have our share in this country, are extremely troublesome to the general planter. While these can be sweetened and purified to a considerable extent by drainage and deep subsoiling, there always remains a certain amount of saliniferous matter in the subsoil which will produce failure in the results of planting, if care be not taken to plant only such trees as are known to withstand its injurious effects.

For the guidance of my readers then, I give a list of trees of this character :—

Acacia Pycnantha.—(Bentham.)...........	" Broad-leaved Wattle."
Ailanthus Glandulosa—(Desf.)	" The Tree of Heaven."
Cupressus Sempervirens.—(Linne.)	" The Common Erect Cypress."
Cupressus Sempervirens Horizontalis—(Miller.)	"The Common Horizontal Cypress."
Eucalyptus Gomphocephala—(Candolle.)	" The Tooart Gum."
Ficus Macrophylla—(Desf.)	" Moreton Bay Fig."
Lagunaria Patersoni—(Don.)	* * *
Pinus Radiata—(Don.)	" The Radiated Cone Pine."
Pinus Halepensis—(Ait.)	" The Aleppo Pine."
Pinus Maritima—*(Syn. P. Pinaster.)*	" The Maritime Pine."
Robinia Pseudo-Acacia—(Linne.)	" The Common or False Acacia."
Tamarix Gallica	" The Tamarisk Tree."

~~~❧❀❧~~~

CHAPTER XXXII.

Trees Suitable for Street Planting.

THIS list applies wholly to the planting of single rows of trees along the streets of cities and towns, for shelter and shade to the footpaths.

Although I hope many more kinds will be added to the list within the next few years, as we come to find out the species which will grow in our climate, the following can in the meantime be relied on as being suitable for the purpose :—

Melia Azedarach	"White Cedar."
Platanus Acerifolia	"Maple-leaved Plane."
Ulmus Suberosa	"Cork Elm."
Ulmus Montana	"Scotch Elm."
Ulmus Campestris	"English Elm."
Ficus Macrophylla.	"Moreton Bay Fig."
Ailanthus Glandulosa	"The Tree of Heaven."
Robinia Pseudo-Acacia	"The False Acacia."

CHAPTER XXXIII.

Trees Suitable for Planting on Calcareous Soils.

There is a great deal of what is known as "limestone country" in this colony. On such spots, care should be taken to plant those kinds of trees only which are known to grow well in soils of this character. Of the trees given in Chapter XXVII., the following are suitable for planting in calcareous soils:—

Acacia Decurrens—(Willd.)	"The Black Wattle."
Acacia Dealbata—(Link.)	"The Silver Wattle."
Acacia Pycnantha—(Bentham.)	"The Broad-leaved Wattle."
Araucaria Excelsa—(Brown.)	"Norfolk Island Pine."
Cedrus Deodara—(Loudon.)	"The Indian Cedar."
Cupressus Sempervirens—(Linne.)	"The Common Erect Cypress."
Cupressus Sempervirens Horizontalis—(Miller.)	"The Common Horizontal Cypress"
Eucalyptus Gomphocephala—(Candolle.)	"The Tooart Gum."
Eucalyptus Leucoxylon—(Mueller.)	"South Australian Bluegum."
Eucalyptus Odorata—(Behr.)	"The Peppermint Gum."
Ficus Macrophylla—(Desf.)	"Moreton Bay Fig."
Frenela Robusta—(Cunn.)	"The Native Pine."
Grevillea Robusta—(A. Cunn.)	"The Silky Oak."
Lagunaria Patersoni—(Don.)	* * *
Pinus Halepensis—(Ait.)	"The Aleppo Pine."
Pinus Pinea—(Linne.)	"The Stone Pine."
Robinia Pseudo-Acacia—(Linne).	"The Common or False Acacia."
Schinus Molle—(Linne.)	"The Pepper Tree."
Sterculia Heterophylla—(Beauv.)	"The Flame Tree."
Tamarix Gallica—(Linne.)	"The Tamarisk Tree."

CHAPTER XXXIV.

Trees and Shrubs Suitable for Hedges.

UNDER this heading I give a list of those plants which may be grown as hedges in the colony, with the sites suitable for each, and their mode of culture.

CRATAEGUS OXYACANTHA.—*Linne.*
(The Hawthorn.)

Grows best on deep rich loamy soils. It succeeds in this climate only in our ranges and cooler regions. The seed (or haws) should be rotted in sandy soil until the pulp is removed, and then sown thinly in nursery rows. The young plants should be transplanted out into rows for one year before they are removed for hedging purposes.

LYCIUM HORRIDUM.
(The African Box Thorn.)

This grows well on the plains. It may be cultivated on the line of fence either by sowing the seed or transplanting the young plants from the nursery lines.

MACLURA AURANTIACA.—*Nutt.*
(The Osage Orange)

Requires a good deep loamy soil and some degree of shelter. Deciduous; makes a good hedge.

Grow in nursery and transplant out afterwards when the plants are one year old.

ULEX EUOPAEUS.—*Linn.*
(The Whin, or Furze.)

Sow the seed on the line of fence. Keep trimmed up, and a good hedge will be the result. Will grow on any kind of soil.

TREE FENCES.

For the high close hedge of lopped trees, referred to in Chapter XXIV., I recommend the following trees :—

Populus Fastigiata........................ " The Lombardy Poplar."
Eucalyptus Rostrata .... " Redgum."
Eucalyptus Leucoxylon .... " S. A. Bluegum."
Eucalyptus Globulus .... " Tasmanian Bluegum."

LIGUSTRUM VULGARE. *–Linne.*
(The Privet.)

There are several species and varieties of the *Ligustrum*, all of which make beautiful and excellent hedges.

These can be easily propagated from cuttings, and transplanted into the line of fence when one-year old plants.

OLEA EUROPAÆ.
(The Olive.)

Makes an excellent hedge. Grow from seed and rear plants in the nursery.

ROSA RUBIGINOSA.—*Linne.*
(The Sweetbriar.)

Cultivate by the seeds sown on line of fence. With care and attention this makes a fairly good hedge fence.

ACACIA.—*Armata.*
(The Kangaroo Island Acacia.)

Sow seed on the line of fence. Keep well trimmed up, and a good hedge will be the result.

TAMARIX GALLICA,—*Linne.*
(Tamarisk Tree.)

A good hedge plant. For description and mode of culture, see page 101.

CHAPTER XXXV.

Trees Suitable for Planting on the Sea-coast.

The trees mentioned below will be found to thrive well on or near the sea-coast :—

Acacia Pycnantha—(Bentham) .... " The Broad-leaved Wattle."
Casuarina Quadrivalvis—(La Billardiere) . " The Sheaoak Tree."
Cupressus Sempervirens Horizontalis (Miller) " The Common Horizontal Cypress"
Cupressus Sempervirens—(Linn) .... " The Common Erect Cypress."
Eucalyptus Gomphocephala—(Candolle) .. " The Tooart Gum."
Pinus Pinaster.—(Ait) .... { " The Cluster Pine ;" or,
Pinus Maritima .... { " Maritime Pine."
Pinus Halepensis—(Ait.).............. " The Aleppo Pine."
Pinus Austriaca—(Hoss.) .... " The Black Austrian Pine."
Pinus Laricio—(Poiret.) .... " The Corsican Pine."
Pinus Radiata—(Don.) .... " The Radiated Cone Pine."
Robinia Pseudo-Acacia—(Linn.) .... " The False Acacia."
Tamarix Gallica—(Linn.) .... " The Tamarisk Tree."

www.ingramcontent.com/pod-product-compliance
Lightning Source LLC
Chambersburg PA
CBHW030846270326
41928CB00007B/1244